POLITICAL VANITY

POLITICAL VANITY

ADAM FERGUSON ON THE MORAL TENSIONS OF EARLY CAPITALISM

MATTHEW B. ARBO

Fortress Press
Minneapolis

POLITICAL VANITY

Adam Ferguson on the Moral Tensions of Early Capitalism

Cover image: Photo of plaque of Adam Ferguson on his gravestone in St Andrew's Cathedral cemetery/Kirsten Brorson

Cover design: Laurie Ingram

Library of Congress Cataloging-in-Publication Data

Print ISBN: 978-1-4514-8275-1

eBook ISBN: 978-1-4514-8439-7

The paper used in this publication meets the minimum requirements of American National Standard for Information Sciences — Permanence of Paper for Printed Library Materials, ANSI Z329.48-1984.

Manufactured in the U.S.A.

This book was produced using PressBooks.com, and PDF rendering was done by PrinceXML.

To Ashli

Your support was not in vain.

CONTENTS

Introduction

They speak of human pursuits, as if the whole difficulty were to find something to do: they fix on some frivolous occupation, as if there was nothing that deserved to be done: they consider what tends to the good of their fellow-creatures as a disadvantage to themselves: they fly from every scene, in which any efforts of vigour are required, or in which they might be allured to perform any service to their country. We misapply our compassion in pitying the poor; it were much more justly applied to the rich, who become the first victims of that wretched insignificance, into which the members of every corrupted state, by the tendency of their weaknesses, and their vices, are in haste to plunge themselves.

— Adam Ferguson on the "Corruption Incident to Polished Nations"[1]

"They," "they," "they," "they." Adam Ferguson's ardent repetition raises the natural question of just *who* "they" might be. His conclusion to the passage offers a clue, of course, but the reader of Ferguson's *Essay* would by this point already have known who the "they" are. His concerns have been made plain; the "rich" are identified explicitly as those citizens who actively forsake political (especially martial) participation in favor of opulent passivity. He has in mind, perhaps, the polished gentry who wish to flaunt publicly the true extent of their private leisure. Yet his criticism of the indolent and bored seems to apply even more broadly and appositely as it extends across the centuries between his time and ours. Presently, "they" could represent almost anyone, regardless of wealth. The rhetorical humor of Ferguson's colorful pronouncement is a fruit of its prophetic poignancy. His frustration imparts wisdom late-moderns can readily identify, and thus we glimpse here a flicker of what is to come, both for our inquiry into Ferguson's moral and political thought-world, as well as for his pronouncements upon modern commercial society. The "they" he chastises as pitiable may in many respects include late-modern societies within that broad third-person plural!

1. Adam Ferguson, *An Essay on the History of Civil Society*, ed. F. Oz-Salzberger (Cambridge: Cambridge University Press, 1995), 246.

1

This narrow example captures the wider, more generic aim of the essays that follow: to work our way conceptually inside Ferguson's mind and allow his insights to illumine contemporary questions. For the purposes of this introduction it would be best to start on the wider view and taper incrementally, contextualizing each step along the way till we reach Ferguson himself. As a means of provisional orientation, the central question of this book takes the following line: What kinds of moral and political tension did the reorganization of economic goals introduce to early-capitalist societies? Each chapter will in turn take a different approach to this question by focusing on Ferguson's dominant theoretical interests—history, action, and political institutions. To understand why the period, place, and people in question merit our attention and to set the stage for the chapters to come, it would be useful to take preliminary account of *why* our inquiry has settled on this particular conceptual territory. Why is eighteenth-century Scotland an optimal context for this study? What makes Adam Ferguson most appealing? If moral and political implications of early-capitalist societies are of foremost interest to this inquiry, readers may ask, why focus on a comparatively neglected theorist of eighteenth-century Scotland?

First, why eighteenth-century Britain? This particular period of British history is unquestionably among its most distinguished. Intellectually and culturally the nation pulses with enthusiastic expectation. The popular feeling was that the country had made a political and social turn of sorts, entering a favored position historically and a new era of civil liberty; the Glorious Revolution, union of parliaments, and fiscally secure Hanover monarchy achieved over a twenty-year period also doubly reinforced this sense of stability and promise. On an economic plane, stability is the fertile soil in which commercial life is rooted and hope is the water that continually nourishes it. Stability and hope mutually foster one another in the garden of society. With this growth we find, unsurprisingly, sustained and notably widespread discussion of economic policy.

The self-fortifying nature of the stability-hope duality heralds a shift in the way politics is contemplated in the eighteenth century: from consideration of *governmental* modalities to consideration of politico-*economic* modalities. Political thought of the sixteenth and seventeenth centuries had been largely concerned with questions of authority, order, and functions of government; now the tide has shifted, and weighing most heavily on the mind of eighteenth-century Britons is the authority, order, and function of political economy. Yet it is still reflected upon as a subject of *philosophic* interest. Political economy had not yet been mathematized and would remain a subject of prudent deliberation, not of quantification. By late century, however, especially after the publication of Adam Smith's *Wealth of Nations*, the primacy of philosophy in commercial theory would begin to give way, but not until. That gradual transition was aided by increased acceptance of a Newtonian world-picture. "Natural" theories and designations enter their ascendancy and eventually subsume the discipline of philosophy itself to pure natural authority. By the mid-eighteenth century "natural" authority had also become the rubric of political economy, and political economy in turn had become the supreme demonstration of natural authority. This mutual self-justification would have its most significant impact on how the organic relation between private pursuit of wealth and public pursuit of justice was understood. Division between public and private collapses in the economic sphere and the two are consistently assumed to co-mingle; that is, private commercial pursuits are viewed as publicly advantageous, just as public pursuits would be viewed as privately advantageous. Thus, the reasons for Britain's importance during this period are threefold—a popular sense of entering a new political era of liberty, a shifting of attention from governmental to politico-economic modalities, and a breakdown of divisions between private pursuit of wealth and public pursuit of justice.

The interesting question was not *whether* God appointed political authority, but *how* that authority was to be lawfully wielded. A notion like "covenant," for example, lingers in theological debate for much of the eighteenth century, especially when those debates skirt political intrigue, but with the additional freight of Lockean contract, as though the two were synonymous. This contractarian formulation of political authority runs theoretically parallel to vehement advocacy for the divine right of kings as fundamentally providential. The issue of divine right and social covenant were, however, but two strands of a much broader eighteenth-century debate over the nature and function of providence itself. Newtonian world-pictures threw metaphysics into disfavor and initiated revisionist theories of natural law, virtue, and even redemption. With time it would become difficult even to distinguish a philosopher's appeal to "providence" from his appeal to "natural law." Natural law seemed to capture empirically the providential mode. The deist threat had not yet fully materialized and would not until the turn of the century. Questions of God's immanent activity in the world bore directly on the basic religious experience of every believer: if God's will is expressed most elegantly in the natural law, then how is one to grasp the experience of God? Terms like "superstition" and "enthusiasm" emerged as referential pillars of ecclesial debates surrounding this very question. For the "superstitious," experience of God is mediated through sacraments, icons, relics, or pilgrimages, or else anything that might channel spiritual communiqués. Enthusiasm, on the other hand, referred to the direct and unmediated physical experience of God, recognizing sensual receptivity through (sometimes bizarre) bodily displays as the climactic validation of divine privilege, sometimes to the point of equivocating worship itself with corporeal enjoyment of God.

As a generic summary of these theological debates, we might say that the tendency was to reimagine the old in light of the new and to identify divine *telos* or commandments with the experience of natural law. Creation under human dominion gradually improves and progresses, and the original, all-sustaining power keeping civilization on its stadial course is the natural law. The tradition of faithful Christian obedience to divine commands artificially narrows to pure conformity with the physical demands of natural law achieved through moderation of passions. The binding authority of law and government likewise condenses into empirically verifiable patterns of how the world works and, in particular, how societies unite and prosper. The tendency in eighteenth-century theology is to clarify what God accomplished in his initial creative act by interpreting contemporary circumstances as decisive expressions of his potential intentions.

Theology thus becomes worldly in all the wrong ways. Providence is natural law established by the faculty of reason. The world appears to operate in such-and-such a way and to such-and-such an end, and by these appearances is duly judged as natural or unnatural, providential or artificial. What emerges from this view is a concept of providence *identical to* human judgments upon advantages or benefits arising from the intellect, civil society, or natural world. If something seems advantageous or beneficial to me, to civil society, or to the natural world, then that thing or event must be providential, seeing as *every perfect gift is from above, coming down from the Father of lights with whom there is no variation or shadow of turning* (James 1:17). And it is precisely in light of this understanding of providence that what had traditionally been considered wrongdoing within the Christian tradition could on this account become a Godsend. Envy and covetousness, for example, become viewed as essential to social cohesion and instrumental to the machine of industry. Righteousness, the other side of this polarity, becomes viewed as conformity to law, a masculine virtue approved and conferred by the public. Sin and righteousness are reinterpreted by many theorists of the period in a way categorically detached from their Christian origin or content. Sin is no longer a transgression against God, but an injury to the accepted norms of public happiness. Righteousness is no longer associated with salvific grace, or the heart of God, but with conformity to the erected standards of institutions and customs.

Maneuvering sin and righteousness into new positions meant that justice, too, would require realignment, which often took the form of conceptual subordination to the possession of property. By making property a condition of justice—indeed its very starting point—an instrument of commerce dislodged justice as a traditionally overarching political authority. Justice becomes defined in terms of distribution and a definite lack of temperate moderation. Ironically, this notion of justice was by no means all-inclusive. Some, like George Turnbull, viewed equality as idealistic and utopian, while others, including Hume, depicted equality as a viable political goal inspired by extensive commercial growth. By 1764, although ranks in society were seen as essential to its lasting cohesion, theorists could not at the same time resist the enchantments of equity and thus slipped into the unavoidable tension of advocating a necessarily stratified society and its endless pursuit of equality. Viewed *historically*, this was not a tension in the slightest. The progressive advancement of humankind through the ages is a story of superseding economic epochs. For Hume and Smith, concepts like justice and authority are themselves shaped by the overwhelming momentum of commercial improvement and thereby lead civil society to a state of affairs in which commerce *precedes* political authority as a commanding power. Divine providence is viewed within this conjectural model of history as a more or less redemptive and sanctifying power. Such a notion no doubt reflects certain commitments to Christian orthodoxy—to make right and to make holy, for example—but is not an adequately discriminating account of providence. *What*, exactly, is God redeeming? What *kind* of improvements can or should be rendered? Here the meaning of history becomes a story of an inevitable future, where refinements seek only further refinements, luxuries still greater luxuries, and innovations to still higher innovations. This progressive improvement, readers are told, is ultimately what makes one happy.

As a point of clarification, the ascendance of natural authority to theoretical supremacy did not at the same time subvert habits of framing political questions in broadly theological terms. In fact, doctrines of providence remained the centripetal force of eighteenth-century theology, as is evident in the innumerable attempts to reconcile the idea of God acting immanently within a closed Newtonian world. Natural theology now required natural foundations and natural legitimacy. One of the overarching tasks later in this book, however, will be to rebut the popular characterization of the eighteenth century, particularly of Britain, as an age of enlightened deism. Isolated figures, like Samuel Clarke, obviously entertain certain deistic commitments, but as will be seen later there is no reason to consider this the dominant or even popular theological point of view.[2] Details of that argument will be rehearsed later. For now I wish only to note that philosophical inquiry of the period retained theological shape and did not altogether jettison its Christian heritage. Arguments were still required to show some degree of theological fidelity, even if the object and method of philosophy had become "natural" and less "revealed."

Having offered a few qualifications for the question of "why eighteenth-century Britain?" it would be useful now to consider the narrower question of "why Scotland?" As a point of clarification, this question does not mean to include the whole of Scotland, but primarily southern Scotland and its vibrant port towns. The term "vibrant" is a particularly apt description in this regard, since Scotland had benefited richly from the constitutional changes inaugurated at the century's turn by the union of parliaments.[3] The country had prospered politically and economically under these new constitutional arrangements and this would lead naturally to an enrichment of philosophical reflection. Of course, Scotland's philosophical tradition was already of some repute; the new commercial confidence enjoyed at midcentury simply gave this tradition its needed relief and leisure. Naming a few members in this talent pool vividly illustrates the nation's philosophic eminence: Gershom Carmichael, Francis Hutcheson, David Hume, Adam Smith, Henry Home (Lord Kames), Thomas Reid, George Turnbull, George Campbell, Hugh Blair, James Beattie, Alexander Gerard, Dugald Stewart, Adam Ferguson, and a host of politicians and armchair intellectuals trained in the humanist arts.[4]

By the 1760s and '70s Scotland had become the epicenter of philosophical engagement and, significantly, almost all the names included in the list above dwelt in Edinburgh at one time or other, some permanently. Edinburgh was *the*

2. Characterization of this century as an age of enlightened deism has been repeated most forcefully by Charles Taylor in both *Sources of the Self* (Cambridge, MA: Harvard University Press, 1989) and *A Secular Age* (Cambridge, MA: Harvard University Press, 2007). Karl Barth intimates similarly in the first chapter of *Protestant Theology in the Nineteenth Century* (London: SCM, 1972). On a separate track, many intellectual historians have utilized this presumption of latent deism as a sign of democratic replacement of hierarchical structures, whether ecclesial or civil. See, for example, "Scepticsm, Priestcraft, and Toleration," in *Cambridge History of Eighteenth Century Political Thought*, ed. M. Goldie and R. Wolker (Cambridge: Cambridge University Press, 2006) and J. G. A. Pocock, *The Machiavellian Moment* (Princeton: Princeton University Press, 1975). An alternative interpretation of the "long eighteenth century" that I follow closely throughout this book is J. C. D. Clark's meticulous study in *English Society: 1660-1832* (Cambridge: Cambridge University Press, 2000). For an example of the deism mentioned above see Samuel Clarke, *The Works* (New York: Garland, 1978).

3. A brief retelling of the unification story is offered at the end of chapter 1.

4. Francis Hutcheson, of course, immigrated to Scotland from Ireland, which may also serve as testament to Scotland's wider philosophical attraction.

place to be for intellectual stimulation.[5] As a city of much notoriety, achieved through the help of a new constitutional order and political consciousness, Edinburgh serves as an intense microcosm of the period's unique cultural fixtures. Given this cultural activity it is therefore unsurprising that improved economic conditions would prompt philosophers to contemplate the nature of political economy itself. How were circumstances once so dire—failed colonial charters, domestic famine, constant threats of rebellion—commercially transformed in less than three decades? Scotland, and Edinburgh in particular, promptly became the locus for working out how the nation and city became a commercial success story, and its philosophers would interrogate the material causes of commercial growth with matchless ability and breadth. We must not forget, moreover, that these are immensely practical theorists who wish to understand why life is lived as it is and how its conditions might be improved upon. Such commonsense practicality explains why it proves so difficult to find an essay of the period falling outside the disciplines of history, morals, or politics—the objects considered are socially constructive.

So, of all places, why is Scotland a site of such tremendous intellectual activity? Its unique commercial advantages stimulated a new political consciousness that would lead naturally to a concentration of philosophical reflection on political and economic questions of the day. The Scottish Enlightenment is, after all, an exceptional phenomenon indebted to political stability and organized around philosophical personalities, making it an ideal setting for examining the moral and political tensions of early capitalist societies. How capably the philosophies emerging from these circumstances were reinvested into Scottish life is touched upon indirectly in chapters 2 and 4.

Of those distinguished Scottish philosophers listed above, why select Adam Ferguson as a principal conversation partner for this study? The question, in fact, gives rise to another that is perhaps more important: Why, exactly, has he remained so inconspicuous? Why is he a *surprise* selection? This thesis offers a litany of reasons why he should not have been so marginalized by modern moral and political historiography and situates him, alternatively, among the earliest modernity critics. Perhaps he has been marginalized or overlooked because his criticisms did not, as it were, "win the day." Either way, it is the cautious subtlety of his thought, the sheer radiance of argument resistant to the popular tactics of British moral and political theory, that makes him an extraordinary figure of the period. Where his peers are optimistic, he is often

5. Edinburgh's intellectual prominence was arguably preceded historically by Aberdeen and Glasgow; however, Edinburgh's establishment as the nation's capital and bastion of political intrigue ultimately sanctified it as a place of substantive intellectual activity.

pessimistic; where his peers see wealth, he sees slavery; where his peers see progress, he sees decay. Indeed he tended regularly to see things his own way.

To get a better sense of his general placement within the wider tapestry of eighteenth-century Scotland it would useful here to offer a few brief biographical remarks.[6] Adam Ferguson was reared in a Kirk minister's family on the invisible Perthshire border between the Scottish highlands and lowlands. His position of birth, both familially and geographically, would prove crucial to his professional career, affording him a rigorous classical education and advantageous connections to the nobility. By the time of his matriculation to St. Andrews in the early 1740s he spoke both Gaelic and English fluently—an ability that would later secure his placement as chaplain to the Black Watch—and was steeped in Greek and Latin classics. Completing his St. Andrews degree at nineteen years of age he then relocated to Edinburgh to continue studies in Divinity. Here he would forge lifelong friendships with churchman peers and receive his first introductions to modern philosophic methods. His studies would be cut short, however, by a hastened appointment to the 43rd Highland Regiment (Black Watch) as deputy chaplain. A Gaelic-speaking ordinand of exceptional ability with Hanoverian sympathies proved the ideal candidate for such a strategic post. His *Sermon in Ersh* delivered to the Watch on the eve of the '45 Rebellion is a marvelous example of midcentury political theology.[7] He intended to accept ministry of a Kirk parish outside Edinburgh after decommission from the Watch, but a failed application and the death of his father in 1754 eventually forced him to accept an offer as tutor to a young Scottish lord on continental tour. Upon return to Scotland, Ferguson inadvertently entered a tumultuous shifting of social and ecclesial tides. He swiftly became engrossed in civil debates over militia policy and Kirk debates over the morality of stage plays—in particular, the public scandal surrounding the "*Douglas* affair." Although he would eventually lose the debate over establishing militias, his support of stage plays on moral and biblical grounds held sway by making it clear that the arts both form and disclose the character of civil society simultaneously.[8] By positioning himself on the side of his friend and *Douglas* playwright, John Home, Ferguson joined the swelling ranks of what has been described as a group of Scottish moderates.[9] Their

6. All such remarks are derived from Jane Fagg's invaluable biography of Ferguson in *Correspondence of Adam Ferguson, Vol. I*, ed. V. Merolle (London: Pickering & Chatto, 1995), xix–cxvii.

7. For an introduction to and transcription of this *Sermon* see Matthew Arbo, "Adam Ferguson's Sermon in the Ersh Language: A Word from 2 Samuel on Martial Responsibility and Political Order," *Political Theology* 12, no. 6 (2011).

8. Adam Ferguson, *The Morality of Stage Plays Seriously Considered* (Edinburgh: 1757).

victories here and on future issues would alter the course of many theo-political Kirk trajectories.

Ferguson's appointment as Advocates Librarian in early 1757 at David Hume's recommendation would be the first step in a long and distinguished academic career. Roughly two years later, and again at the recommendation of Hume, Ferguson was appointed to the Chair of Natural Philosophy at the University of Edinburgh. This appointment brought to rest temporarily his many years of wandering and confirmed his academic, not ministerial, vocation. This appointment and confirmation did not halt his faithful service to the church, for he served continually as an elder and Assembly representative throughout the 1760s and '70s. In any event, it was not until his appointment to the more fitting Chair of Pneumatics and Moral Philosophy that he published his more reputable treatises, which include *An Essay on the History of Civil Society* (1767), *The History of the Progress and Termination of the Roman Republic* (1783), and *Principles of Moral and Political Science* (1792). Each of the texts was well received at the time of their publication, though it would be the *Essay* that ultimately secured his reputation in the history of political thought. Socially, Ferguson was very much the man about town, involving himself with various societies and supporting strategic political causes. He was a coveted conversation partner described amiably by all who knew him. Political involvement would eventually secure his invitation to join the Carlisle Commission as a negotiator to the recently victorious American colonies. But having failed even to make an appearance before the Continental Congress, the Commission returned to Britain just in time for Ferguson to fall terribly, almost fatally, ill. He resigned his chair shortly after recovery and retired to the countryside to try his hand (yet again) at farming the Scottish borders. Eight years later, at the age of seventy, he embarked on a long-awaited trip to the continent for his induction into the Berlin Academy of Sciences and subsequent leisure tour of Italian states. Returning to Britain he farmed his plot on the borders countryside another ten years before admitting, at age eighty-seven, that he had become too feeble to maintain his estate and would retire to St. Andrews for its convenient proximity to family. Adam Ferguson died there on February 22, 1816, aged ninety-three, and was buried in the old cathedral grounds along the northern wall. His unusually long, energetic, and eclectic life tells a great deal about the sort of person we are listening to—a practical man with practical concerns, whose ideas and sensibilities are derived from concrete

9. Richard Sher, *Church and University in the Scottish Enlightenment* (Edinburgh: Edinburgh University Press, 1985). For the general purpose it serves, the term ("moderate") more or less works.

experiences of political life. At different junctures in life Adam Ferguson was a classicist, chaplain, tutor, traveler, librarian, elder, professor, diplomat, farmer, and socialite. The philosophic and contextual relevance of Ferguson for the central question is suitably assured, for he speaks to the question when and where it first arose.

Interrogating the moral and political tensions of early-modern commercial theory at the point where standard policy and procedure began to be called into question can isolate and illumine crucial ethical questions emerging from the present configurations of our economic order. In the course of this study it will become evident that some of these questions are perennial, while others remain unique to the eighteenth-century Scottish experience. Be that as it may, the broader contours of arguments considered here can directly inform moral deliberation over the theological origins, means, and ends of modern economies. Now, having said that, it is equally essential that some indication be given as to *how* this historiographic program will be conducted. To prevent entanglement in overly complex methodologies, Adam Ferguson has been enlisted as a conversation partner and guide. Every attempt has been made to grasp the questions and circumstances through his eyes, empathizing with them when possible, engaging the figures he engages, and familiarizing with his way of seeing. In other words, the goal has been to understand what Ferguson would speak to contemporary states of affairs were he given the chance.

Three additional qualifications of some recurrent tactical decisions would be helpful at this point. First, modern thinkers who do not necessarily "belong" to the eighteenth-century world are consulted periodically. Martin Heidegger, Hannah Arendt, Robert Spaemann, and Reinhart Koselleck, for example, make occasional appearances to demonstrate why Ferguson's problems are not entirely unique and to help build an interpretive framework for understanding what is theoretically at stake. Connections between such thinkers and our eighteenth-century subjects will vary in strength; sometimes the connection will seem tacit or loose, while at others more direct. In every case, however, the aim is to widen momentarily the picture we are considering to include voices that may help us better understand it.

Second, there is the matter of eighteenth-century literary styles. In this age, concision and elegance are united to the enhancement of both. John Locke and David Hume are notable stylistic exemplars in this respect; their prose transmits lucidity in every turn of phrase. Well-placed irony is utilized with greater regularity and confidence, and very typically adorned in elaborate idioms. Aptitude for stretching sentences to their maximum potential also seems to have been especially prominent in the long eighteenth century. Often the relief of arriving at a sentence period feels not unlike coming up for air at the end of an underwater swim! Such length, along with the necessary support of seemingly innumerable clauses, makes the task of quoting these figures with brevity inordinately arduous. I have therefore adopted the technique of breaking quotations into parts so as to convey the intended argument as clearly and succinctly as possible without losing the passage's fundamental spirit. Leaving these passages intact would require disruptive block quotes, robbing the essay of momentum.

Third, and lastly, allow me to qualify the use and non-use of certain economic terminology. Despite Adam Smith being heralded as the father of modern economics, and despite the Scottish Enlightenment's role as incubator of early capitalism, the word "capitalism" as an economic signifier does not appear in the literature treated by this thesis. Neither does the term "economy" for that matter. The transliterated *œconomy* makes rare appearances here and there, harkening to ancient notions of household management and agricultural trade, but its eighteenth-century application lacks the conceptual freight of contemporary references. "Commerce" is their word of choice and I have tried to follow them in using it, though, admittedly, the terms above are also occasionally employed when most fitting to the case. This care with economic terminology has been equally applied to other conceptual genres.

This book aims to contextualize Ferguson's philosophical contributions historically, bring his preoccupations to the foreground, and affirm his defense of Christian metaphysics. Chapter 1 is largely an exposition of Ferguson's philosophy of history. It begins with a brief rehearsal of his Scottish peers' understanding of historical progress and concludes with Ferguson's critique of conjectural models. Special attention is given in this chapter to the relevance these models have for growth variables in modern economics. Chapter 2 is also predominantly expositional, outlining in detail Ferguson's theory of action. As before, the aim is to distinguish him from his contemporaries and to demonstrate how his theory of action squares with certain Christian commitments. Particularly interesting on his account is the negative impact of much commercial practice upon human initiative and political exertion. In chapter 3 I focus almost exclusively on Ferguson's moral and political critique of popular economic policy advanced in his *Essay*. His preoccupation with establishing militias remains central to his wider political hermeneutic, for as the defining issue of his early political pamphlets it applies to the troublesome corroboration of commerce and militarism outlined in the *Essay* itself. Upon rehearsing these arguments I then apply Ferguson's pessimistic conclusion to contemporary economic realities. Lastly, in chapter 4, I identify three of

Ferguson's metaphysical opponents—determinacy, universality, and romanticism—and affirm his suspicion that when incorporated philosophically each distorts an authentically Christian vision of reality and the moral order upheld by it.

Each chapter of this book builds upon the next to support something like the following argument: The goals of modern commerce and the methods used to achieve them generate irresolvable moral and political antinomies—to the extent that modern economies remain inherently progressive—by inhibiting or altogether eliminating authentic human action and by undermining the very political institutions intended to sustain commercial life. The several premises supporting this conclusion are articulated in each chapter. If the poignancy of Ferguson's judgment occasionally takes the reader by surprise, you are not alone; it serves as testimony to how little has changed since the late eighteenth century and thus the moral contradictions of the modern marketplace speak as truthfully to our perils as they did three hundred years ago to the Scot. This poignancy will repeatedly validate the contention that study of a less prominent moral philosopher of the eighteenth century can furnish new insights into questions of immanent relevance for Christian political theology.

If Ferguson can help us ask better ethical questions about modern commercial exchange, then this book will have served part of its purpose. If it persuades the reader that Economy can itself become a tyrant, negating the freedom and abundance it promises always to supply, then it will also have served the other part. The self-defeating nature of modern economy is premised on the antithesis between means and ends—false ends inevitably undermine even the most precise means. And thus an increasing number of "theys" are swept up into the abstract confusion of economic misdirection and left scratching their heads over which exchanges are truly worth transacting and how they ultimately contribute to the common good. Such confusion is perhaps the final product of having misplaced treasure: *for where your treasure is, there will your heart be also* (Matt. 6:21).

1

Ferguson's Political Theology

The aim of this chapter is to better define the Christian character of Adam Ferguson's moral and political thought in preparation for deeper investigations of his thought in later chapters. Bearing in mind that we are not dealing with a systematic theologian but a Christian philosopher, this essay attempts to name moral and political theories *against* which Ferguson is most resistant and critical. Clarifying what he conceptually or practically opposes will share the benefit of highlighting what he positively favors as an alternative, his moral and political concerns being directed primarily at what seem to him perversions (and in some cases *in*versions) of Christian moral and political thought. Opposition to what I describe as three modern idealistic threats—determinacy, universality, and romanticism—will prop the canvas of this moral and political sketch. Precisely what is meant by each of these ideals will be treated extensively below, so I provide here only a few preliminary definitions. By "determinacy" I mean (generally) the necessary and uninterrupted forces of material cause and effect. "Universality" will refer to the human comprehension of reality and the application of universal principles to everyday existence as complete and totalizing. The type of "romanticism" referred to in what follows is more accurately the romantic seeds of freedom, sentiment, and novelty—overcoming of *telos* and custom in history—buried in fertile soils of the mid- to late-eighteenth century. Preliminary definitions carry certain limits, of course, so more flesh will need to be added to these skeletal definitions as the essay proceeds.

For determinacy, a brief rehearsal of early-modern natural law theory discussed intermittently throughout chapters 2 through 4 will furnish a starting point for outlining Ferguson's response to the theory's metaphysical implications. His critique of mechanistic natural law will also apply to our broader inquiry into commercial order. Similarly, for universality, the brand of determinacy emblazoned into modern imaginations sparked new optimism over the mind's intellectual capacities. Determinacy helped established the conditions on which universality could kindle and enflame. Accounting for how this development came about will be an important goal in treating the second threat, as will its bearing on the overarching commercial question. Lastly, for romanticism, after we have noted the ways in which Ferguson is and is not a romantic, the inquiry will then focus on his critiques of two modern impulses: the sanctification of feeling and devotion to political novelty. At the conclusion of this essay, despite not having captured a thoroughgoing theological project, it will be possible to point toward certain theological commitments and in so doing offer a few examples of why Ferguson's thought is relevant to contemporary moral and political debates.

DETERMINACY

The observation that Newtonian physics furnished the eighteenth-century world a reinterpretation of natural law has become common to the point of axiomatic.[1] Prior to Newton, the story goes, natural law remained an expression of divine reason or will (depending on one's view) and treated most intelligibly as a metaphysical subject—"good," "truth," and "right," for example, being terms intrinsically transcendent yet imposing immanently binding powers behind the natural law. Law was considered "natural" in the sense that it corresponded essentially with the way things seemed to go in the natural world, describing nature though not contingent upon it. Early in the seventeenth century and several decades prior to the publication of Newton's *Principia*, Hugo Grotius described the Law of Nature as so unalterable "that it cannot be changed even by God himself."[2] The law of nature is permitted to authorize as it does because

1. The evidence of Newton's theoretical persuasiveness can be glimpsed as early as Locke and gains supportive momentum throughout the eighteenth century, especially in the Scottish Enlightenment, reaching its forceful climax in Kant. Gradual realization in the latter part of the eighteenth century that Leibniz had stumbled onto similar mathematical findings independently only further reinforced the explanatory prowess of Newtonian mechanics. As David Hume would attest, if Newton's theory could overcome the scrutiny of continental theorists, which by the mid-eighteenth century seemed to have already been achieved, "it will probably go down triumphant to the latest posterity." Adam Smith would have even fewer reservations. Isaac Newton, *Philosophiae Naturalis Principia Mathematica* (London: William Dawson & Sons, 1954); G. W. Leibniz, *Philosophical Essays*, ed. and trans. R. Ariew and D. Garber (Indianapolis: Hackett, 1989); John Locke, *Essay Concerning Human Understanding*, ed. P. Nidditch (Oxford: Clarendon, 1975); David Hume, *Essays Moral, Political, and Literary*, ed. E. F. Miller (Indianapolis: Liberty Fund, 1987), 121; Adam Smith, *Essays on Philosophical Subjects*, ed. I. S. Ross (Indianapolis: Liberty Fund, 1982), 91–105; Immanuel Kant, *Critique of Pure Reason*, ed. and trans. P. Guyer and A. W. Wood (Cambridge: Cambridge University Press, 1998).

were God to change or alter his Law it would lead to contradictions implicating divine character. The Creator is a God of order, not of disorder. Passages from Genesis 18, Isaiah 25, and Romans 2 further establish this point, for God himself "suffers his actions to be judged by this rule."[3]

But surely there exists some contingency or flexibility in the Law of Nature—must everything be so rigidly prescribed? No, not necessarily, and Grotius says as much when he contends that "in reality there is no change in the unalterable law of nature, but *only in the things appointed by it*, and which are liable to variation."[4] The law of nature is therefore conceived as an authority, not as a uniform determinant of what does and does not occur or what shall or shall not be performed; it sets parameters to the possible—where an action is performed and how far it might be carried out, for example—but cannot control the action undertaken. This is why, explains Grotius, things are "allowed by the law of nature, not absolutely, but according to a certain state of affairs."[5] Unalterable as it may be, then, the law of nature is at once resolute and permeable, generic and particular, liberating and restrictive. Specific states of affairs, which for Grotius are governed by the Law of Nations, illustrate perfectly how the law of nature authorizes jurisprudence that avoids universal codifications best formulated contextually according to an actual state. Before a law can be considered binding it must first be considered right or truthful, a "dictate of right reason showing the moral turpitude or moral necessity of any act from its original agreement or disagreement with a rational nature."[6] But that is not all. Not only must an act agree or disagree with the right, but each act "is either forbidden or commanded by God, the author of nature."[7] Thus, for Grotius, the law of nature derives its authority from natural right, which is itself an expression of God's authority as author of nature.

Grotius' differentiation between what the natural law *commands* and what the natural law *determines* is in the latter part of the seventeenth century, particularly after publication of Newton's *Principia*, blended into new philosophic formulae. Accounting for this change, one possible explanation is that natural law became theoretically identified with laws of physics, and indeed Newton claimed rather confidently in his Preface to have "cultivated

2. Hugo Grotius, *De Jure Belli ac Pacis*, trans. A. C. Campbell (London: M. Walter Dunne, 1901), book I, chapter 1, section x.

3. Ibid.

4. Ibid. (emphasis mine).

5. Ibid.

6. Ibid. By "moral necessity," Grotius means simply that "the laws of nature must always bind us."

7. Ibid.

mathematics so far as it regards philosophy."[8] This mathematical study of nature and its laws fundamentally altered the way natural law was comprehended. Language of mechanism came to replace the organic unity of the natural law seen in its parts and whole, in its universality and particularity, in its transcendence and its immanence. Scrutiny was leveled most stubbornly upon the perfections of creation, where God sent forth the world with such order that powers generating and sustaining this order were eligible for quick identification and comprehensive description. From this newly erected rational platform humanity could scrutinize all the principles, rules, and forces establishing existence. Newton's mathematical vision subsequently relegated the unseen powers of the world to descriptive analysis of cause and effect: such-and-such a phenomenon is explained by formula "X," and so therefore the variables of formula "X" identify both the cause and rationale of the phenomenon under consideration. Determinacy and necessity were thus embedded within the very texture of the natural law.

Philosophers were coming to terms with the implications of Newton's mechanistic world picture as late as the mid-eighteenth century, ruminating once again over the perennial opposition between necessity and freedom. Laws of nature impose determinacy on reality by categorically disallowing states of affairs to be in any way other than they are, the present state being simply the effect of a seemingly infinite chain of prior causes. This raises the obvious question of whether there is any room for contingency, spontaneity, newness, creativity, or basic human liberty. Hume famously rekindled Scottish fascination with this seasoned dilemma on Newtonian terms. Both in his *Treatise on Human Nature* and later in the *Enquiries*, he maintains that while matter is always uniformly determined by cause-and-effect relationships, human beings remain susceptible to the determinants of nature because "man is everywhere the same" and "we acknowledge a uniformity in human motives and actions as well as in the operations of the body."[9] Each person's will is directed by passions that animate it. Interpreting and understanding human action presupposes certain degrees of uniformity and regularity. Predictability helps ensure rational consistency. Every will has some passion or motivation behind it rendering the effects of some prior cause. "Liberty," quips Hume, is not entirely unlike "chance, which is universally allowed to have no existence."[10] He thus employs descriptions of material cause and effect to close

---

8. Isaac Newton, *Mathematical Principles of Natural Philosophy*, trans. Robert Thorp (London: 1777); see first sentence of Preface.

9. David Hume, *Enquiries Concerning Human Understanding*, ed. P. H. Nidditch (Oxford: Clarendon, 1988), 83–84. See also *Treatise on Human Nature*, ed. P. H. Nidditch (Oxford: Clarendon, 1978), 399–422.

the already narrow window for metaphysical freedom. From here he applies determinacy to other academic subjects, like history and political economy, and allows for material mechanisms to describe metaphorically how each is configured around certain causal relationships. Add to this the determinist leanings of other eighteenth-century theorists, and the perception that the spirit of the age favored physical determinacy is vouchsafed.

Ferguson's resistance to this spirit of determinacy takes several trajectories. We shall see in chapter 3 that the best way to describe his account of freedom is dialectical: freedom is best expressed in rightful limitations and rightful limitations are best expressed in freedom, belonging to one another as each makes the other intelligible to itself. Unbound freedom is not unlike the irrational thought of playing football without sidelines or field judges, or of a swim meet without starting guns or lane assignments—actions require a defined place and convention for performing *some*thing rather than *any*thing. On the social plane, "limitations" refer to physical and political laws establishing concrete human domains; "limitations" are referred to in the eighteenth century as natural laws. For Ferguson, the jurisdiction of natural law (understood in the Grotian sense) sets the parameters within which every state of affairs cogently obtains but underdetermines what must or must not be the case in every such state of affairs. Law's scope is decided by the general contours of nature and, most importantly, by nature's Author. Nature is a *creature*, after all, and as a creature it expresses something about the character of its Artificer. "All of nature is connected," Ferguson explains, "and the world itself consists of parts, which like the stones of an arch, mutually support, and are supported."[11] This order of nature "consists in movements" that counteract, disturb, regulate, and balance one another; appearing to humankind as though nature repeatedly oscillates between being at peace with itself, and being at war. Yet "what seems to be irregular is the perfection of order," so any disturbance introduced to this oscillation is but part of nature's exquisite form. Nature has an integrity, an internal coherence. If one wishes to say it is governed by "laws" that would be fine with him, so long as the description did not abolish meaning or violate the Author's character.

Early sections of the *Principles of Moral and Political Science* argue repeatedly that although not everything is within one's freedom to choose, each nevertheless has distinguishable options from which to decide. So, for example, one cannot choose which society to be born into, but afterward may choose

10. Hume, *Enquiries*, 96.

11. Adam Ferguson, *Principles of Moral and Political Science* (New York: Garland, 1978), 18.

who to make friends with or keep company. What sets man apart from other animals is that he possesses a mind "intimately conscious of itself, as it exists in thought, discernment, and will."[12] In section thirteen of chapter II of the *Principles*, moreover, determinacy is countered by positive appeal to the truth of metaphysical freedom. Freedom is implicitly acknowledged in the fact of each being *conscious* of her freedom. If one is conscious of one's freedom, believing it to be the case that one's actions bear the mark of contingency is evidence for being free in reality. Putting even greater distance between himself and Hume, he asserts that "effect is correlative to cause, and they are inseparable; but there may be existence without any cause external to itself, as there may be will without any cause but the mind that is willing."[13] The mind, not the passions, energizes and directs the will; it is "the cause of its own determination." Therefore "it is absurd," as he sharpens the rhetoric, "to consider volition as an act of necessity, not of choice."[14] Philosophical clarity on this question was made opaque by the employment of "mechanical imagery" to describe how existence formally operates. In point of fact, will is by definition the "direction of mind" and therefore allows only such determinacy as might allow for meaningful expressions of human freedom. "Discernment and freedom are essential to intelligent beings."[15]

"Mechanical imagery" has also been misapplied to divine providence. "The consideration that infinite power must have preordained the operations of will, and that these operations therefore cannot be free, is an argument taken from a collateral subject," says Ferguson; an idea that would seem to undermine the fact that we are conscious of freedom. By "collateral subject" he means (presumably) that of divine omniscience. Human beings cannot know with any certainty what divine omniscience is like or to what it ultimately extends. We *do* have a notion of our own freedom, however, and this seems more reliable of the pair. This is not to say that God's knowledge is somehow limited, for it includes "whatever may result from the source of contingence" and "his almighty providence is sufficient to control the effects of such freedom."[16] Ferguson's proposal departs slightly from Augustinian compatibility of divine foreordination and human freedom in its suggestion that necessities of divine foreknowledge would still be perfect even if that knowledge allowed for certain "contingencies." God sees in the "eternal Now," but our consciousness of

---

12. Ibid., 48.
13. Ferguson, *Principles*, 153.
14. Ibid.
15. Ibid.
16. Ibid., 154.

freedom must imply that we are not self-deceived. Freedom must therefore survive as a provision in foreknowledge itself.

Were we not free, how could humanity be held responsible for its actions? Determinism dissolves any form of moral or legal culpability into meretricious innocence. Similar problems of culpability arise in instances where motive and will are causally equivocated; if passions empower will, then those passions motivating the will become the objects of blame, not the action or actor. On this Aristotelian view one can always declare after committing a wrongful act that "I'm not yet the kind of person who can avoid X or positively perform Y" and escape guilt. Motive determines will to the erasure of fault. "[H]ow absurd," remarks an annoyed Ferguson, "for the fatalist to plead that he is not accountable for having committed a bad action; under pretence that his intention itself, which was the motive or cause of such action, was bad!"[17] Therefore neither humanity nor the reality it inhabits is wholly determined by material causes or divine foreknowledge.

Resisting the determinacy latent in "mechanical imagery," Ferguson posits instead a God of wisdom whose will is not exhausted or comprehended by the laws of nature. Human action contains a wild surplus of meaning that once performed discharges a multitude of consequences uncontrollably into the world that often "discover a meaning as an effect discovers a cause."[18] All action emerging from divine government is ripe with significance and power. If semblances of ingenuity or innovation are detected in any human accomplishment "the wisdom of God," not the person or species, is to be credited.[19] God is envisaged as coming alongside the mind, supplying it with virtues and needed insight. So, human action upheld by divine wisdom would seem to open certain contingencies, suggesting a more "organic" and less mechanistic government of reality.[20]

Ferguson therefore rejects material determinacy on much the same grounds as Grotius. The laws of nature are *authorities*, not comprehensive physical determinants. In saying what is or is not the case, the laws of nature also define what can and cannot be the case. After Newton, the laws of nature and the divine will are more or less equivocated, and the resulting brand of determinacy contains two crucial implications for eighteenth-century thought. On the one hand, equivocating divine will with natural law enshrines any event

---

17. Ibid., 155.

18. Ibid., 38.

19. Ibid., 53.

20. Ferguson can be seen throughout the *Principles* to draw upon "organic" imagery deliberately opposed to "mechanistic." See especially Part I, chapter 3, section xiv and Part I, chapter 1, section i.

or idea as God-breathed. Newton's German counterpart, Gottfried Leibniz, had suggested that because God could do no other than create the best of all possible worlds this world must in fact be the best possible, for "if the smallest evil that comes to pass in the world were missing in it, it would no longer be this world."[21] This is possible because God has "ordered all things beforehand once for all, having foreseen prayers, good and bad actions, and all the rest."[22] The "pre-established harmony" of the universe presumes all experienced evils to be a necessary part of God's original creative act. And we will see in chapter 2 why Scottish theorists were inclined to accept the basic material determinacy, or "pre-established harmony," of Western history, and parse it into four eras of commercial innovation. Determinacy was transposed retrospectively onto the narrative of history itself, reinterpreting it as a saga of material and rational progress.

When the purposes of God were conflated with the natural law and the story of history retold as a narrative of material progress, it is perhaps inevitable that God's intentions would soon be considered *in terms of* material progress. Commercially speaking, as will be seen in chapter 4, determinacy was so fundamental to market logic in the eighteenth century that the laws of nature were identified with the express will of God. Economic man functions in such-and-such a way, as do the patterns that result over a period of time, and therefore when supported by the great history of economic innovation even the injustices and evils of the market are sanctified by ends the market pursues. Indeed, the professional study of modern economics itself has become in the modern age a study of models comprised essentially of variables. Use of the word "variable" is a bit of misnomer, of course, since economic models depend on conceptualizing even indeterminate signifiers to get explanatory equations off the ground. Modern economics dismisses indeterminacy, in other words, because as an essentially mathematical discipline it is premised on fixed and determined variables of commercial information, actions, and events.[23] It is precisely this brand of determinacy that disallows spontaneity, uniqueness, altruism, nonconsumptive political action, and other potential defeaters to the "triumph of determinacy" that Ferguson opposed so adamantly.[24] He opposed it, I suggest, because determinacy draws upon a *pagan*, not a Christian conception of human existence; an alien political theology that confuses how the world

---

21. G. W. Leibniz, *Theodicy*, ed. Austin Farrar, trans. E. M. Huggard (London: Routledge, 1952), 128.

22. Ibid.

23. The developing field of Behavioral Physics proves rather troubling in this regard; as though human action could be predictable enough to fit within alphanumeric variables of mathematical certainty.

24. A. O. Lovejoy, *The Great Chain of Being* (New York: Harper & Row, 1960), chapter 7.

participates in the life of God. It is not enough to say forthrightly that creation is given perfect license to be what it is—it must also give account for how it fails to exist in the *right way*. "Providential deism," as Charles Taylor has defined the period in question, might refer to an *emerging* school of thought in the long eighteenth century, but he mistakenly assumes it to be the *dominant* view of eighteenth-century philosophy and theology.[25] To better understand how this version of determinacy found support and migrated into commercial theory more broadly, we turn our attention to the next conceptual "resistance" on which Ferguson sets his sights: Universality.

UNIVERSALITY

When I suggest Ferguson resists universality I certainly do not mean to imply that he rejects universals or that he is not a realist; he undoubtedly is. Universals are real and objects in existence refer to them—or depending on one's view, are supported by them—when truth claims are under consideration. Belief in the existence of God, for example, is thought to be universal.[26] "Principles" of universality, on the other hand, are truths that do not depend upon human comprehension to be authoritative. Principles contain ideas that operate like axioms, anchoring and integrating other ideas to which they relate. But their truth is not person-dependent. Ferguson has no problem with the objective existence and authority of universals; indeed they are necessary. His concern is rather with *claims* of universality, as in the presumption to have achieved universal scope. His critique of universality is therefore largely epistemic in orientation—the principles adhere in reality but the hurried claiming and application of unjustified principles should be resisted.

The spirit behind Ferguson's resistance to empirical certitude was later given a more penetrating and critical focus by Hegel, in whom we can see the persistence of Ferguson's reservation. The *Phenomenology* begins by treating consciousness in much the way Ferguson has treated the more generic concept of mind, as something to *apprehend* but not to *comprehend*.[27] Sense-certainty,

25. Charles Taylor, *Sources of the Self* (Cambridge, MA: Harvard University Press, 1989), part III. See also *A Secular Age* (Cambridge, MA: Harvard Belknap Press, 2007).

26. "The belief of the existence of God has been universal," Ferguson claimed in one of his lectures, "and cannot depend on circumstances peculiar to any age or nation, but must result of human nature, or the suggestion of circumstances that occur in every place and age." See *Institutes of Moral Philosophy* (New York: Garland, 1978), part III, sections 1 and 2.

27. G. W. F. Hegel, *Phenomenology of Spirit*, trans. A. V. Miller (Oxford: Oxford University Press, 1977), 58. In our review of Hegel we are concerned here only with his critique of what we have called

Hegel explains, might appear the richest and truest kind of knowledge, but on reflection we find that "this very certainty proves itself to be the most abstract and poorest truth."[28] Sense perceptions are not immediate truths chiseling away at the mind's *tabula rasa*. "An actual sense-certainty is not . . . pure immediacy, but an instance of it."[29] For Hegel, universals are located in the *particular*, where essence and instance synthesize to open the universal door. Sense certitude is never immediate but always mediated—universals colored with a particular hue. History is the site of this dialectic as it tells the story of incarnate universality. Ferguson would affirm the historical site of this dialectic perhaps, but would resist the eschatological implications Hegel's historical "spirit" conveys. As we have referred to its eighteenth-century mode, at any rate, universality represents a perspective claiming rational completeness in a world teeming with incompleteness, ambiguity, tension, and paradox.

Anyone who has lived long enough to grasp the paradoxical balance of intelligibility and confounding chaos in the created order, with its seasons and vicissitudes, is aware "he cannot define knowledge, nor tell what it is to know, any more than he can tell what it is for the mind to exist."[30] In its pithiest formulation, skepticism calls into question claims of noetic certitude on the grounds that "knowledge" is itself unknowable. One cannot describe adequately even what it means "to know," and so one's conception of things is described alternatively in terms of "ideas" forming images, types, or copies resembling originals. Challenging our understanding of what ideas are and how they are acquired is the limitation of language's reliance on analogy and metaphor, in which representation of "impressions" of originals can only draw upon illustrations of how original ideas are "copied" intellectually. In short, "we cannot have knowledge of a subject if we have not any notion of it."[31] Behind every piece of knowledge are notional preconditions that make knowledge possible—grammatical rules, linguistic customs, logic, and so forth. These preconditions are equal parts linguistic and conventional.

In his most focused treatment of knowledge, "On Knowledge in General," Ferguson seems to have a mind to reject the whole fledgling project we have come to call modern epistemology. The theoretical impetus to explain comprehensively the mind and its content is essentially mistaken, he thinks,

"universality"—the claiming of rational certitude and absolute rational scope—not the doctrine of universals within Hegel's vast system.

28. Ibid.

29. Ibid.

30. Ferguson, *Principles*, vol. I, 70.

31. Ibid., 74.

"and hence the scepticism of ingenious men."[32] The mind's inexplicability resonates with the eighteenth-century discipline of "pneumatics," which when defined by its etymological roots signifies something akin to "*spirit* of the mind." Immaterial, intangible, and incomprehensible, when made the direct object of study the mind shrouds itself in mysteries. Now, of course, there is no sense in denying the reality of knowledge *en toto*, particularly if everyone were cautious "neither to admire nor condemn what they do not know."[33] The epistemic complication Ferguson wishes to avoid is the claim to have *explained* the mind's complexities; our methods should seek only to "investigate and to apply, not to explain, the laws of conception and will."[34]

Ferguson opposes undue rational optimism inasmuch as it appears as a recurrent theoretical proviso of the period, and to grasp the force of his reservation more completely, we can summarize with three concepts: rational immediacy, noetic certitude, and the exaltation of ideals.[35] The first, rational immediacy, relates to impressions made upon the mind through experience. Material experience leaves an immaterial mark on the perceiving mind. The second, noetic certitude, supposes that one's beliefs are held naturally with complete certitude. These conclusive beliefs are then leveled definitively upon reality in ways expressed by the third theme, as an exaltation of ideals. Certitude precipitates the eventual consecration of ideals, replacing the governing order of reality with the intellectual principles achieved through scientific evaluation of experience. The three conceptual themes are therefore collaborative. Ferguson's response to this joint subordination of metaphysical authority to rational comprehension is most sharply addressed in his treatment of the "fundamental law of morality" in chapter two, part two of the *Principles*.[36] The moral significance and effect of this subordination was what Ferguson found most problematic and helps explain his positive attempt to underscore the metaphysical, and indeed *religious*, character of morality.

Eighteenth-century moral philosophy concentrated on the interior constellation of affections causally enlivening morality. Beginning with Shaftesbury's invention of the Moral Sense and continuing through Hutcheson, Smith, and Hume, moral authority became ever more narrowly defined by

---

32. Ibid., 76.

33. Ibid.

34. Ibid.

35. The transition Ferguson opposes is what at least one modern commentator has referred to as the dissolution of reality into subjectivity. Hannah Arendt, *The Human Condition* (Chicago: University of Chicago Press, 1998).

36. As will be seen, the argument is also reiterated in several sections of the *Essay*.

intellectual capacities or faculties, the moral "sense" itself becoming but a super-added function similar to that of smelling, tasting, or touching. Moral deliberation thus became a natural, inferentially immediate function; learned from birth, ingrained by society, and refined by attention to public perception. At the time of Ferguson's appointment to the Chair of Moral Philosophy at Edinburgh, both Smith and Hume had already sought to reduce morality to a conceptual singularity—"fellow-feeling" and "sympathy" respectively. In Smith's case we have but to note that his text on moral philosophy is cast in terms of a *Theory of Moral Sentiments*, which seems to suggest the subject and object of morality are one and the same. Hume's *Treatise* and *Enquiries*, and to a lesser extent his *Essays*, elevate the passions to the highest plane of moral theorizing. Smith and Hume's mistake, at least on Ferguson's view, was to understand sentiment and reason as separable, one as capable of moral evaluation and the other as amoral. Emphasizing sentiment led Smith and Hume to devote most of their attention to development of a reenvisaged virtue ethic naturally framed in terms of habits and customs. What raises alarm on this account is the extreme internalization of moral authority and privileging of human judgment. As will be seen later in this essay, affections furnish the spring sunlight that nurtures a budding romanticism.

For Ferguson, on the other hand, *benevolence* is the fundamental law of morality. All virtues that have ever been named, especially the classical virtues of wisdom, fortitude, temperance, and justice, converge at a conceptual starting point of ultimate meaning—benevolence. He often refers to benevolence as though largely synonymous with "goodness," or a "good-will" (its etymological root), since the "greatest good incident to human nature is the love of mankind."[37] This love serves as the platform for all the other virtues and aids each person's attempt to observe them in their conduct. "Benevolence, therefore, may in some degree be considered as a principle of wisdom, of fortitude, and temperance; and . . . we cannot greatly err, in assuming it the fundamental or primary object of moral law."[38] Establishing love as the chief moral good of humankind and the unity of the virtues, we perceive already the beginnings of a thoroughly Christian, and perhaps more acutely Augustinian, account of ethics.[39]

37. Ferguson, *Principles*, vol. I, 110. The reader may find it initially peculiar that Ferguson refers to the "greatest good" as love of mankind, rather than the love of God. Why he does not need to refer to love of God in this passage will become clear later.

38. Ibid., 111.

39. For an excellent review of Augustine's political ethics, see Eric Gregory's *Politics and the Order of Love* (Chicago: University of Chicago Press, 2008).

He treats "applications" of the moral law as if it were a scientific exercise. This "science" of morality "abstracts from local forms and observances" and "becomes in the mind a principle of extensive benevolence, by which the individual states himself as part in the order of nature, and entirely devoted to the will of its Author."[40] It is worth noting that "science" is nowhere defined by Ferguson as the embodiment of scientific *method*, but rather as a lens through which to clarify perception of the created order. Skepticism chastens science only lightly, for it is to him "the highest attainment of created intelligence and nearest approach to a communication with the supreme Creator."[41] As a discipline it "contemplates the form of beauty," putting one in touch with the substance of creative brilliance. *Moral* science is applied to reality, seeing as it is vastly "more obvious to most men than even the qualities of mind itself."[42] If this reductive science is applied subjectively rather than objectively; that is, if we apply moral interrogation strictly to the interior moral life, then moral "science" becomes precisely what Hume insists—a "science of man." Sentiments, affections, passions, and other internally nonrational powers are now cultivated in the scientific Petri dish. Whether such interior powers are "approved" or "disapproved" thus becomes a serious moral problem. What sorts of criteria, for example, can measure the moral worth of affective powers? Why do we praise or blame others for what they do?

The challenge of accounting for moral approbation persists throughout the eighteenth century, and Ferguson is quick to demonstrate just how many voices have given credence to it. Clark, Shaftesbury, Kames, Smith, and Hume are all shown to have occupied themselves with this question of why we are inclined to praise or blame others, and for what reason. Ferguson thinks it should not matter whether we find another's conduct morally pleasing or odious, but whether certain actions are in fact either *right* or *wrong*. "Mankind are not agreed" on what actions are to be praised or blamed, and "they differ no less in what they admire than in what they enjoy."[43] According to his interlocutors, virtues and the approbation resulting from them are reflected in an action's congruence with excellence or perfection. Yet, he rejoins, "mankind are not agreed on this subject," for "the idea of perfection no doubt may be associated with subjects divested of merit."[44] His concern is that ideal standards of perfect virtue will be wrongly assigned to actions that are, in truth, largely or entirely

40. Ibid., 113.
41. Ibid.
42. Ibid.
43. Ibid., 134.
44. Ibid.

immoral. "External actions" may result from any number of internal conditions of mind variously "different in different instances" and therefore not universal. The reason why "there is not any certain rule of approbation or disapprobation respecting the manners or behavior of men" is that "the same physical action in one instance applauded as a virtue, in another instance is reprobated as a crime; or rather . . . where the physical action is the same, the moral action is altogether different and is an object of approbation or disapprobation, corresponding to that difference of the moral quality."[45] There is often an enormous chasm, as it were, between what an action really accomplishes and what one *thinks* an action accomplishes. What is in one place commended as an act of bravery might in another place receive condemnation for foolishness, and Ferguson gives examples of how widely and frequently this ethical tension has appeared in history, but the problem is not merely one of moral reality and faulty perceptions.

The moral content of an action is mostly formed by the general customs of a people, such that what is "mannerly" in one place might be an "offense" in another. Local context is imperative to moral ascription. The tension introduced by this turn to contextual assessment vexes us because "we are not qualified to perceive in what manner the moral action . . . should be differently *understood*, or in what manner the same moral action should result from physical performances extremely different."[46] Attributes admirable or detestable may vary greatly from place to place and from person to person; people may simply have different opinions on the commendations due an action when many "actions of men are considered more as *expressions* of what they mean or intend, than as operations materially beneficial or hurtful."[47] In either case, whether considering the consequences or the intentions of an act, complications are induced by misinterpretation. For Ferguson, however, regardless of how intentions or consequences are interpreted, the truly benevolent agent does whatever *bene-fits* the world around him, since it is in fact "beneficent to treat every person in the manner which he himself conceives to be beneficial or kind."[48] Opinion does not alter the rightness or wrongness of an act, which altogether overrides what anyone may think of it, because differences of opinion "will be equally found not to affect the original or the essential distinction of moral right and wrong."[49] This distinction leads him to the

45. Ibid., 138.
46. Ibid., 140.
47. Ibid.
48. Ibid., 141.
49. Ibid.

attractive conclusion that disagreements over approbation are in reality disagreements about the "use of words, not in conceiving the distinctions of right and wrong."[50] The crucial issue, then, is that the principles of approbation do not assist in discerning the moral propriety of an action and so should be jettisoned in favor of the more holistic evaluative tool—rightness.

Defending his flank against the looming charge of relativism, he offers clarification by reminding us that the first law of morality designates "the love of mankind as the greatest good to which human nature is competent."[51] Every society is aware of moral principles corresponding with those of other societies and so therefore constitute a "rule" by which each may judge the meaning or significance of an action. This "rule" is the Rule of Propriety. Its elegance as a rule is displayed in its talent for permitting certain contextual distinctions while at the same time disallowing total rejection or ingenious recasting of moral principles. It applies efficiently to cases great and small, personal as well as social. The endurance of propriety is supported by its inherently customary nature, ensuring definite continuities with history. Custom buttresses the authorial potency of the Rule. Customs illumine but do not determine the Rule, just as the Rule illumines but does not determine customs.

And yet, what are we to do when customs violate the Rule of Propriety? How are the potentially contradictory claims between custom and the Rule to be arbitrated? The Rule applies "wherever the manners of our country are dangerous to its safety or have a tendency to enfeeble or to corrupt the minds of men; to deprive the citizen of his rights; or the innocent of his security; it is our duty to do what is for the good of our fellow creatures, even in opposition to the fashion and custom of the times in which we live."[52] When custom and right no longer correspond in certain particulars, the task of society becomes one of correcting injustices, to *righting* wrongs.

Ferguson seems to have understood the biblical command to love thy neighbor, as have many Christian theorists in history, to imply a universal obligation. This duty consists in the *command* of God as an expression of his will. Aristotle's virtue ethic, for example, cannot provide the same exemplary moral guidance, because the very idea of striking a mean between extremes is misleading: a "proper mean" is derived conceptually "from a previous knowledge of what is right."[53] In fact, to pursue the middle course between two extremes is to have chosen the course of mediocrity for mediocrity's sake. Does

50. Ibid., 148.
51. Ibid., 149.
52. Ibid., 154.
53. Ibid., 157.

an extreme version of justice or right exist? How might it do so? What are its salient features? Merit and demerit are properties attributable to *mind*, which can exercise itself excellently or ignorantly but never encouraged to perform what is mediocre. Wisdom, goodness, temperance, and fortitude are all characterized as "excellences" of mind. Ferguson locates merit in the mind proximately because external actions "do not appear to be vested with any moral quality, until the movement performed is traced to its connection with the disposition of mind from which it proceeds."[54] One cannot judge of the conditions in another's mind and so cannot ascertain whether praise or blame is due.

But if others cannot decide merit, how then is it decided? His response points toward history and to God's governance of it; thinking historically about a moral action demands that "qualities of mind" and "movements of the body" be "combined together in the conception which men mutually form of their moral distinctions."[55] As we have seen, only history can tell us about what man is capable of performing and what the shape of his moral obligations might be. Actions *disclose*, or "imply," certain qualities of mind, bringing to expression previously unseen or unknown interior powers. With this proposal he demonstrates acute biblical awareness, for "wherever wisdom and goodness exist, proper and beneficent conduct will follow, as the tree produces its fruit" (Matt. 7:17).[56] Wisdom and goodness are "approved [on their own account] as constituents of perfection and happiness."[57]

If the Moral Law is defined by its "expression of what is good," to what does the moral law owe its authority?[58] Obligations and sanctions endowing the moral law with binding force are derived from the command of God: "the Sovereign of the universe, by having made things as they are, has given his command, and promulgated his law in behalf of morality; and in every instance of conformity to his law, and in every infraction of it, continues to apply the sanction of happiness and misery."[59] Doing moral good is an act of obedience to the divine command. It is an act done happily, for one can be assured that the command requires what it does precisely because it makes ultimate happiness possible. To obey the law of love apart from any sense of goodness would be to fall short of the command, since it would not be out of love for God that the action was undertaken. So much then for Kant's call to observe duty for

---

54. Ibid., 165.
55. Ibid.
56. Ibid., 166.
57. Ibid.
58. Ibid., 168.
59. Ibid., 171.

duty's sake. Religion and morality cannot be separated—they "share in a *genuine alliance*":

> [T]he wisdom and goodness, which we perceive to be the constituents of happiness, are likewise enjoined by the Sovereign command of God. They are presented to our thoughts, as attributes of the Supreme being himself, and as forming in him the objects of reverence and love; and our own capacity attaining, in any degree, to *a participation of these qualities* is considered as the highest perfection or prerogative of our nature.[60]

Humankind enjoys wisdom and goodness to the extent that it participates in the life of God, who reveals his character to guide moral deliberation. From the person of God proceeds the authority of his government extending both to the mind and to the actions of humanity, restraining "not only the overt acts of iniquity, but even the thoughts, wishes or purposes which may lead to such external effects."[61] Indeed, asks Ferguson rhetorically, "In what is the love of God different from the love of goodness itself?"[62] In positing this question he makes explicit the link between the essence of the law—goodness—and the God in whom it consists. Diverse principles, rules, and laws of morality therefore receive their authority exclusively from the command and person of God.

Universality is attributable only to God, for it is only by God's goodness that the disclosure of law instructs the human mind. Judgment is a cumbersome power for humans to wield, simultaneously overwhelming and supportive of the moral life as such. Ferguson's account of Christian moral philosophy demonstrates why moral authority cannot be grounded in any human faculty. Knowledge can be a notoriously elusive animal. "Under the highest measures of conviction, which attend our perception of things, truth does not appear to be necessary; and the reality may be different from the appearance that is perceived by us."[63] Such contingencies invite us to relinquish our claims to certitude. History proves repeatedly that items cherished as most integral to the social order often pass into the twilight of disfavor as quickly as they arrived. Morality cannot be reduced to sentiment or custom—or, in truth, to the rational adjudication of causes—because morals in their continuity cannot be bound to either power. Sentiments and customs can be false, unjust, or even immoral, but

---

60. Ibid., 172 (emphasis mine).
61. Ibid., 176.
62. Ibid.
63. Ferguson, *Principles*, vol. I, 83.

in suggesting that morals are vested in the right and true as decided by God, Ferguson deflects the self-same charge of universality. He avoids it because the universality he claims is not human in origin or cause. One has only to attempt a search for moral prescriptions within Ferguson's writings, a sermon and invitations to love notwithstanding, to realize that one is dealing with a moralist who understands the uncontrollable relation he shares with the moral order. Each must live life in deference to the true and the right—to obey and to act in rightness. This is best observed by studying the annals of history, which is why his *Essay* maintains as one of its dominant themes an overt difference between the changeable and the unchangeable. "Rude" nations and "polished" nations are not rude and polished by virtue of their customs, as was so popularly asserted throughout the eighteenth century, but by virtue of their actions in service to the public. Error remains an open possibility to which all humanity may succumb.

What does a dialectical confrontation between determinacy and universality bestow in its synthesis? This question is not easily answered. One reason for its difficulty is that romanticism contains within itself the conceptual synthesis of this dialectic only *in part*; that is, romanticism is not the product of this synthesis but the descriptive heading it belongs to—romanticism, as it were, *envelops* the synthesis. So, we require a more rounded picture of romanticism's eighteenth-century form. Like determinacy and universality, romanticism also interrogates the natural order of things but with broader function, operating more as an arbiter of the frustrated antagonisms between determinacy and universality. Before venturing into the philosophic thicket of romanticism, however, a few remarks are needed on just what is meant by the term "romanticism" and what ways Ferguson is or isn't romantic himself.

ROMANTICISM

The truth or falsity of "romanticism" as a signifier depends on what kind of "romanticism" is being contemplated. If a "plurality of romanticisms" adhere in society (as has been suggested by scholars seeking paradigms for interpreting the romantic impulse) then the success of my claim that Ferguson resists "romanticism" will invariably depend upon what *kind* of romanticism is being considered.[64] What is the precise nature of the romanticism Ferguson finds

---

64. Arguments for a "plurality of romanticisms" are found in A. O. Lovejoy, "On the Discrimination of Romanticisms," in *Essays on the History of Ideas* (Baltimore: Johns Hopkins University Press, 1948). For a more recent and historically attentive contemporary treatment of romanticism, see Michael *Löwy* and

problematic? Are there elements of early romanticism he finds worth accepting? From his biography we know he adored poetry, participating regularly in readings, and that the intensity of his literary appreciation provoked him to vehement support of John Home's much-maligned play, *Douglas* (more on the "*Douglas* affair" below). He retired to the countryside of Peebles to try his hand at farming while still very much in intellectual form, presumably for no other reason than that the challenge intrigued him. He even wrote a seminal history of *The Progress and Termination of the Roman Republic*, an effort some have interpreted as displaying certain romantic tendencies.[65] In contemporary use the term is thrown about as though synonymous with lamentable "nostalgia" over a long-lost past.[66] Thinking deeper about the etymology of Romanticism one might also be inclined to associate it with adoration of all things antiquarian and, of course, Roman. This is not an unattractive inference, but eighteenth-century thought contains a great deal more romantic potency than is attached solely to an appreciation of classicism.

Ferguson's thought certainly displays romantic appreciations for the moral and political significance of antiquity. "Rome" was a laudable and grand idea invariably lost because Roman citizens had forgotten what it *meant* to be Roman: "In proportion as the character of Roman citizens lost its consideration and its consequence, the name was easily communicated to all the subjects or natives of any province."[67] Empire building motivated by the accumulation of riches created the conditions that brought the honor and glory of Rome to embarrassment and ruin. Personal felicities of each citizen were transferred to the grandeur of Caesar and state: from happiness derived from personal excellence to happiness derived from national fame and fortune. Ferguson is "romantic" in his view of ancient Rome as offering an illuminating contrast to modern principles of moral and political order. The idea of Rome—its blindness, ambition, structure, opulence, law, and spirit—receives a balanced presentation mindful of both Rome's failures and its successes. Antiquity teaches us something about how to live morally and politically with our neighbor.

Robert Sayer, *Romanticism Against the Tide of Modernity*, trans. Catherine Porter (Durham, NC: Duke University Press, 2001).

65. Adam Ferguson, *The History of the Progress and Termination of the Roman Republic* (Edinburgh: Bell & Bradfute, 1825). Ferguson's *History* was remarkably well received and used regularly as an early-education text on the history of the Roman Empire.

66. On the mistake of reading "nostalgia" (as retrospective longing) into eighteenth-century discourse, see J. C. D. Clark's "keywords" in *English Society 1660-1832* (Cambridge: Cambridge University Press, 2000).

67. Ferguson, *Progress and Termination*, 391.

Ferguson's defense of John Home's stage play, *Douglas*, also reveals romantic partiality. His brief pamphlet *The Morality of Stage Plays Seriously Considered* responded to the anxious opposition of Kirk clergy by rebutting their claim to theatre's morally insidious nature. His argument is almost comically adroit. Stage performance, he begins to tell us, has been in cultural currency for well over two hundred years, and measuring just how corrupting the effects of theatre have been in the course of these two centuries is not easily determined. Britain is perhaps average by comparison, with good and bad men being found mixed in every age and place. His three principal arguments in favor of the stage are as follows: if the stage is morally poisonous, then the effects are slow to manifest; heroic portrayals in stage performance may in fact correct moral missteps; and lastly, these moral exhortations can also purify stage production itself.[68] Essential to all three arguments is their moral perceptiveness. Opposition to the stage cannot be wrought from scriptures that do not expressly denounce it. In fact, the Apostle Paul himself seems at least to have been well acquainted with the Greek performances, alluding to them in both Acts 17:28 and 1 Cor. 15:33. The parables of Jesus, too, rouse the imagination. Parables and plays both tell stories and thus make for superior conduits of moral instruction. The novel artistry of theatre can awaken in the skeptical mind an imaginary world where fictitious characters have failed or succeeded when confronted with moral challenges, and advantage to its credit. Edinburgh's stage plays are plays "which excel in moving compassion, which interest an audience in behalf of amiable characters, which give the proper applause to virtue, and treat vice with ignominy and reproach."[69] The stage is therefore commendable if its comedies and tragedies re-create and encourage moral imagination. Plays offer a fresh form of moral education so long as license is not carried too far. Antiquity's zealous adoration of theatre does not go unrecognized by Ferguson, for plays are but natural expressions of a nation's rich civic arts—the fictitious dramatization of real political life. But appreciating Roman political history and the Greek stage is a fairly harmless affection: might something else complicate romanticism's cultured decency?

Ferguson's consideration of *problematic* romantic impulses presents an even more complex picture. Both biographically and theoretically he displays romantic commitments, but there are clearly certain tendencies of eighteenth-century Britain—politically, socially, commercially, religiously—that attract his criticism. The way he describes nature and the natural ordering of reality often

---

68. Adam Ferguson, *The Morality of Stage Plays Seriously Considered* (Edinburgh: 1757).
69. Ibid., 17.

takes the tone of admiration: a nature in constant movement, conducive to life, intelligently balanced. He admires nature but does not adore it; nature is given intellectual prominence, but not primacy. Ferguson *resists*, though occasionally with unconscious tension, the following three romantic themes: a supposed state of nature, political novelty and rebellion, and the sentimentalization of morals. We will also want to note conceptual oppositions generated by the elevation of nature to ultimate authority. But before interrogating Ferguson's romantic hesitancies it is essential first to sketch conceptions of nature prevailing in the modern period.

In seeking to define "nature," modern minds tend to gravitate toward the scientific bastions of biological and physico-mechanical categories. That is simply how the modern imagination has been formed. Scientific method and the atomistic reductionism it gave birth to and now fosters objectify nature to the point of numbering its constituent electrons. Water is not nature's life-blood, for example; it is H_2O. Nature is reduced to a vast network of bio-electrical reactions tamed from oblivion by still more bio-electrical reactions. But the term "nature" designates vastly more than the relations between electrical charges and chemical compounds. Philosopher Robert Spaemann has recommended a double meaning for the term: "on the one hand, it refers to the origins of things, to what comes first; on the other, it refers to norms and purposes, criteria by which to evaluate our projects, actions and situations."[70] The term's meaning has also been shaped by its adjectival opposites, like "artificial," "voluntary," "historical," and "customary." Eighteenth-century theories of nature had been profoundly shaped by the Newtonian and Leibnizian law-abiding cosmos—nature as all-encompassing—and viewed every event as a result of some previous natural cause. Even someone like Hume, who at least hoped to retain some remnant of custom in his speculations, could not avoid (eventually) relegating nature to "patterns" of natural occurrences taken to be natural laws.

In the eighteenth century, therefore, "nature" is totalizing; "the *un*natural means the same thing as the impossible."[71] Early-modern fascination with the mythic state of nature illustrates the pervasiveness of this comprehensive and reductionist viewpoint. Nature was consequently stripped of its intrinsic *telos* and assigned new goals authorized by nature's purely empirical tendencies. The supposed "state of nature" was held in stark contrast to "civilization"—pure

70. Robert Spaemann, *Essays in Anthropology*, trans. G. de Graaff and J. Mumford (Eugene, OR: Wipf & Stock, 2010), 75.

71. Robert Spaemann, *Happiness and Benevolence*, trans. A. Madigan and J. Alberg (Edinburgh: T. & T. Clark, 2000), 161 (emphasis mine).

nature versus constructed artifact. The nature–artifact duality furnished philosophers with a comparative dichotomy for moral and political evaluation and thereby formalized the question of whether nature and artifact could be made compatible with one another or remain forever antithetical.

These two romantic appropriations of nature help clarify the substance of Ferguson's critique. He addresses the "double-meaning" of nature, and the relation of artifacts and customs to nature, in the opening section of his *Essay*, "Of the Questions relating to the State of Nature." As a preliminary observation it is of some relevance that he feels he must address the state of nature at the very outset, a priority which hints both at the dominance of contractarian political visions in the seventeenth and eighteenth centuries, as well as to his own reservations about contractarian viability for the modern political order.[72] He refers to the state of nature as a "question" inviting critical response.

Commendation from Hobbes, Locke, Hutcheson, and other contractarians was for political philosophy to reach back into the natural origins of the human species, before the establishment of any artifact, state, rule, or government for society's legitimate *raison d'état*. Against this original state of nature all other contemporary political states would be comparatively judged; the pure, ungoverned realm of necessity and passion. For Hobbes, "the condition of mere nature" is "absolute liberty."[73] Likewise, for Locke, to understand political power or right one must first understand "what state all men are naturally in, and that is a state of *perfect freedom* to order their actions and dispose of their possessions and persons as they think fit within the bounds of the law of nature, without asking leave or depending upon the will of any other man."[74] This state is also a state of equality, "wherein all the power and jurisdiction is reciprocal, no one having more than another."[75] Rousseau's more colorful claim that "man was born free, and he is everywhere in chains" enriches the state of nature's poetic vitality.[76] Each theorist believes firmly that covenants constitute the

---

72. Thomas Hobbes, *Leviathan*, ed. Richard Tuck (Cambridge: Cambridge University Press, 1996) and *Human Nature and De Corpore Politico*, ed. J. C. A. Gaskin (Oxford: Oxford University Press, 1994); John Locke, *Second Treatise of Government*, ed. C. B. Macpherson (Indianapolis: Hackett, 1980); Jean-Jacques Rousseau, *The Social Contract*, trans. Maurice Cranston (London: Penguin, 1968). Occasionally included in this traditional list of early-modern contractarian thought are Montesquieu's *Spirit of the Laws* and Hume's *Treatise*. Alexander Pope's *Essay on Man* (Oxford: Clarendon, 1904) and much of Robert Burns's pastoral poetry would be excellent literary examples of romanticism in this regard.

73. Hobbes, *Leviathan*, 245.

74. Locke, *Second Treatise of Government*, 8.

75. Ibid.

76. Rousseau, *The Social Contract*, 49.

binding force of social contracts—beginning with the family and continuing through the wider commonwealth—and that within a state of nature contracts are based on principles of equality as much as they are on freedom. Hobbes, Locke, and Rousseau all elevate the ideals of liberty and equality within their accounts of the state of nature and enshrine them as foundational insights to social order and political constitutions.

Against this early-modern tendency Ferguson interrogates the "question" of a supposed historical state of nature. He dismisses semi-romantic poets, historians, and moralists who consider past ages radically different from present conditions, whose assumption seems to be that "the first state of our nature must have borne no resemblance to what men have exhibited in any subsequent period."[77] Identifying original qualities of man and expressing the "limits between nature and art" are done simultaneously. Ferguson thus identifies what has been viewed traditionally as one of romanticism's early modern tensions between art and nature.[78] Some political theorists have sought to exalt nature and its impulses to previously unseen prominence, while others have tried to represent man as merely a learning animal or conflicted creature predisposed to perpetual warfare. Yet, the "desire of laying the foundation of a favorite system" has "led to many fruitless inquiries," explains Ferguson, and has persuaded philosophers to form a theory that amalgamates a few admirable traits in an "imaginary" origin in bygone ages.[79] History tells a rather different story:

> [T]he earliest and the latest accounts collected from every quarter of the earth, represent mankind as assembled in troops and companies; and the individual always joined by affection to one party, while he is possibly opposed to another; employed in the exercise of recollection and foresight; inclined to communicate his own sentiments, and to be made acquainted with those of others; these facts must be admitted as the foundation of all our reasoning relative to man.[80]

Notions of a wholly free and equal prepolitical man are complete fiction. No record exists that has not found humankind already gathered in community, united by affections and in communication one with another.

---

77. Ferguson, *Essay*, 7.

78. On this point regarding the art/nature tension in the eighteenth century, see especially Lovejoy's "On Discrimination of Romanticisms," 239.

79. Ferguson, *Essay*, 9.

80. Ibid., 9.

The attempt to trace an imaginary state of nature "through ages and scenes unknown" was Rousseau's historiographic mistake.[81] Man's purest form, on his account, is the isolated and perfectly free individual who has not yet been corrupted by political society and its enslaving demands. Ferguson rebuts this claim by reminding us that humankind has always been found in groups and has always been seen as radically superior to the animals; society indeed appears to be "as old as the individual."[82] The second and perhaps most obvious problem with Rousseau's history is its supposition that humanity does not have the intellectual exposure or capacity to posit an existence radically different from present configurations of reality. When theorists attempt to fill holes in knowledge-gaps by crafting new stories we are immediately clued in to certain practical ambiguities surrounding our everyday experience—especially if that experience is overtly political—and which in turn alerts us to the question of whether another more superior source of wisdom is available to us. If we follow Rousseau's logic we are soon deceived into thinking that current mysteries will be opened by the "wisdom of nature" that discloses the meaning of human events simply by identifying the "operation of physical powers" that produced them.[83] The impulse is therefore naturalistic at heart. Yet the *telos* of natural occurrences is precisely what we typically attribute to God and his creative genius, for that is the true source of mystery and explains why we cannot hope to *solve* the problem of our origins.[84] "We are no longer to search for the source of existence," because we know that mysteries are latent in the creative genius of God; "we can only collect the laws which the Author of nature has established."[85] At best, all we can hope for is some insight into a "mode of providence before unknown."[86]

This point on intellectual humility loops Ferguson back around to the romantic bifurcation of nature and art. Here he states straightforwardly, "art itself is natural to man."[87] From the beginning man appears to be an "artificer

---

81. Ferguson refers here to Rousseau's early essay *Discours sur l'origine et les fondements de l'inégalité parmi les hommes*. See *Discours sur l'égalité* (Cambridge: Cambridge University Press, 1941).

82. Ferguson, *Essay*, 12.

83. Ibid.

84. "The concept of nature is now taken to be anthropomorphic, while the essentially *teleological* idea of things in the cosmos having 'movement in themselves' is understood as the usurpation of a *divine* quality." For more exceptional contemporary engagement with the question of human nature, see Robert Spaemann, *Essays in Anthropology*, trans. Guido de Graaff and James Mumford (Eugene, OR: Wipf & Stock, 2010), chapter 1.

85. Ibid.

86. Ibid.

87. Ibid.

of his own nature, as well as his fortune," and seems to set his will always on invention and contrivance. Human beings are at once complex and simple, "obstinate and fickle," complaining regularly about new innovations and yet "never sated with novelty."[88] Humanity's general predisposition is toward improving its circumstances, to getting the upper hand on otherwise uncontrollable powers of human existence. If any general progression is detected in this regard, it is not rapid or hasty but slow, "like the power of a spring silently presses on every resistance."[89] If nature were consecrated as a moral and political criterion from which to work out our deliberations it would be so consecrated at great expense to crucial deliberative categories. Virtue and vice, for example, must ultimately transcend nature, as must good and evil. Defining the good by its natural appearance results in all varieties of moral and political distortion. Ferguson then presses this division between nature and art further by asking rhetorically if nature and artifact are in fact antithetical: "[I]n what situation of the human race are the footsteps of art unknown?"[90] From the beginning humanity is seen to craft artifacts for the betterment of daily life—innovations of today are but a continuation of a persistent historical theme.

Art does not replace nature, but *cooperates* with nature as it emerges *from* nature. Art is among the means nature uses to preserve itself. God has created the natural order in such a way that it contains within itself the means for perpetuation and flourishing. The Creator likewise affords humans the opportunity to act within that order, but "man may mistake the objects of his pursuit; he may misapply his industry, and misplace his improvements."[91] In light of such errors, how can one judge the rightness of any action according to its natural correspondence? The standard and source of action is found in the heart, where the truth about an action's perfection or excellence is disclosed. In scrutinizing the state of nature one will find that "the proper state of his nature . . . is not a condition from which mankind are forever removed, but one to which they may now attain; not prior to the exercise of their faculties, but procured by their just application."[92] What one believes to be "natural" or "unnatural" is endlessly plastic, seeing as both terms are "least determinate in their meanings."[93] A criterion of "naturalness" can clarify nothing in the moral or political order: "for *all* the actions of men are *equally* a result of their nature."[94]

88. Ibid.
89. Ibid., 13.
90. Ibid.
91. Ibid., 15.
92. Ibid.
93. Ibid.

The very best an idea of "the natural" can deliver is a tradition, convention, habit, routine, or custom that communicates a sense of rudimentary order or stability in human affairs.

These two ways of looking at nature converge politically at the intersection of novelty and rebellion. Rousseau, for his part, did not invite or sanction rebellion *per se*, despite the fact that his disjointed account of human nature and unrelenting emphasis upon the essential "rights" of freedom and equality precipitated a revolutionary spirit that would strangle the whole of France by gripping the neck of Paris. If discovering oneself means one is required to rediscover their instinctual and animalic past, then that could only be achieved (realistically) by removing obstructions, whether institutional or conventional, mitigating the purest human expressions. Ferguson, on the other hand, along with other semi-romantics like Burke and Wordsworth, denigrates violent rebellions as categorically unjustified. His *Sermon in Ersh Language* and short pamphlet *Remarks on Dr. Price's Observations* both deliver pointed critiques of violent rebellion.[95] Recall that in the former, Ferguson takes aim at the supposition that the Divine Right of Kings doctrine can serve as warrant for violent revolt, contending instead that a good political order such as existed in Britain at the time (1750s) should be viewed as a providential gift. In the latter, Ferguson counters a certain Dr. Price's claim that American colonies were correct to reject the authority of the crown under the terms set for it as a colony with a line of argument similar to that of the sermon: the colonies enjoy relative peace and prosperity, and thus claims to injustice—taxation without proportionate representation—do not provide an adequate basis for violent rebellion. In truth, "rebellion, if successful, never knows its limits."[96] Dissenters are nothing but "secret enemies of government."

Ferguson seems therefore to have perceived the threats of American rebellion as a kind of childish tantrum. The colonies had been granted a commercial and political order conducive to the good life and in turn the colonists protest at not having sufficient liberty or equality. So bad was the

---

94. Ibid.

95. Adam Ferguson, *A Sermon Preached in the Ersh Language to His Majesty's First Highland Regiment of Foot, Commanded by Lord John Murray, At their Cantonment at Camberwell, on the 18th Day of December 1745* (London: Printed for A. Millar, 1756); *Remarks on Dr. Price's Observations on the Nature of Civil Liberty, &c* (London: G. Kearsley, 1776).

96. Ferguson, *Remarks*, 42. Several pages later Ferguson concludes that "it is evident that the colonies, actuated by the turbulent principles of their ancestors; some prompted by ambition, others instigated by a restlessness of disposition; some from giddiness, others from illusion, gave rise to this detested rebellion" (68).

situation apparently that "a blush must now overspread the face of every Englishman if ever the Americans are mentioned in his presence by a stranger!"[97] Edmund Burke would of course feel a similar embarrassment for the French in the aftermath of their own revolution a decade later. That same Dr. Price who attracted Ferguson's rebuke would receive an even fiercer one from Burke. If we recall here the "double-meaning" of nature we will notice that for Ferguson (and Burke) convention is the track down which origins must travel—the mediating content between the present and past. Abolishing conventions in hopes of reestablishing the original nature of freedom and equality can never succeed. "Those who attempt to level, never equalize," and in the end, "the gross and complicated mass of human passions and concerns . . . undergo such a variety of refractions and reflections, that it becomes absurd to talk of them as if they continued in the simplicity of their original direction."[98] Even *telos* latent in the original will be mediated by the convention making it intelligible.

Modern philosopher of history, Reinhart Koselleck, has stressed throughout his work the conceptual magnitude of politically objectified novelty in this period. The kind of novelty we are considering is leavened by two historical concepts—"crisis" and "revolution." It was not until the late-eighteenth century that the historical meaning of "crisis" (*krisis*), related conceptually to legal or political actions like "separating" or "judging," was replaced by *events*—and a spirit encouraged by those events—of unavoidable "finality" or "transition." Decision (*krisis*) was replaced by the inevitability of conflicting or changing circumstance: "From the second half of the eighteenth century on, a religious connotation enters into the way the term is used," and this inculcation pervades modern experience "to such an extent that 'crisis' becomes a permanent concept of history."[99] The very meaning of the word "crisis" comes to radically redefine our lived experience. Events of the French Revolution bring this conceptual transition to its climax by presuming that "crisis" had "become the fundamental mode of interpreting historical time."[100] This will not surprise us—the Enlightenment itself is an intellectual precursor to the establishment of crisis. Where at one time crisis brought completion, the crisis of the French Revolution brought only newness.

97. Ibid., 29.

98. Edmund Burke, *Reflections on the Revolution in France*, ed. T. H. D. Mahoney (Indianapolis: Bobbs-Merrill, 1955), 55, 70.

99. Reinhart Koselleck, "Crisis," *Journal for the History of Ideas*, trans. M. W. Richter (April 2006): 370–71.

100. Ibid.

Koselleck refers to this fundamental change in our understanding of time as *Neuzeit* (new-time, or modernity), as seeking "to conceptually grasp what previously was not at all possible."[101] History and *Neuzeit* are in some sense wholly divorced. Time itself becomes parceled into distinct periods—ancient, medieval, and renaissance, for instance—or else thematized by century. Time is broken down into unified coefficients. The French Revolution is the ideal embodiment of this new understanding of time as something to be controlled by human hands. Revolution is the means man has chosen to impose himself upon time, to supersede the old for the sheer pleasure and spectacle of the new. Newness in turn becomes the object of both history *and* future. This idea of modernity beginning with the French Revolution and its new organization of time is doubly supported by the fascinating attempt of French revolutionaries to refashion the annual calendar. Out with the Church calendar, in with the "revolutionary" calendar. The immediate problem presented by this tactic, of course, is that time cannot be comprehended ahistorically. Calendars are themselves based first on the natural cycles of the world, then framed more precisely around enculturated theological observances. But the revolutionaries had nevertheless convinced themselves that "a rationalized nature should ring in a new epoch in history."[102] Calendars emphasize and reemphasize the constant circulation of nature, while the revolutionary insists on the unrelenting newness of time. The meaning of the revolutionary calendar as a historical event is in its judgment (*krisis*) of the Christian calendar, pronouncing upon the past for the sole purpose of future prognosis. Explains Koselleck, "The aspiration to a just order is always already pregiven as that which is to be reborn. To realize a just order thus means to reestablish it."[103] Abolition of the Christian calendar was therefore not only an attempt to replace natural time with rational time, but to replace the centerpiece of time itself—the birth and death of Jesus Christ—in hopes of abolishing the difference between past and future. Meanings of the past are latent in future possibilities. Crisis in the modern age is permanent to the extent that it incorporates eschatology into history.[104]

101. Reinhart Koselleck, "The Eighteenth Century as the Beginning of Modernity," in *The Practice of Conceptual History*, trans. Todd Presner (Stanford: Stanford University Press, 2002), 162.

102. Reinhart Koselleck, "The Revolutionary Calendar and '*Neu Zeit*,'" in *The Practice of Conceptual History*, trans. Todd Presner (Stanford: Stanford University Press, 2002), 151.

103. Ibid., 152.

104. Koselleck refers here to Karl Barth, quoting from his *Commentary*: God is "the origin of the crisis of every objectivity, an origin that lacks all objectivity, the judge, the non-being of the world. The so-called history of salvation is only the continuous crisis of all history, not a history within or parallel to human history."

But revolution is simply the most radical expression of romanticism—a romanticism gone mad. In addition to the open possibility for violent political rebellion to realize the true romantic spirit of freedom and equality, there also subsists within the romantic *ethos* an interior impulse. What I have called the "sentimentalization of morals" found in Shaftesbury, Hutcheson, Hume, and Smith occupies a unique place in this romantic march. The feeling—or passion—behind an action determines the morality of that action and as such implies that "natural" passions be given total expression. What matters morally and politically is the feeling and energy behind actions naturally undertaken. Passions are to this extent *the* fundamental content of morals and thus, to flip the argument around, morals are themselves susceptible to revision in light of what is naturally desired. It is one thing to say that an action must fit within the natural world or ought not violate the natural order; it is quite another to say that whatever is naturally desired expresses moral truth. What concerns Ferguson is not the suggestion that passions have a role in moral deliberation and upon the performance of actions, or that passions cannot be groomed by custom; rather, he takes issue only with *internalizing* moral authority. Translating a previously objective moral order into a subjective set of natural passions, an order judged according to a state of nature that makes the passions truly natural, marks a dangerous turn to the subjective. Passions arising from this impulse toward isolated individuality confuse and fragment the moral order by reducing the rules of civil society to principles protecting personal rights. "Moral sense," "sympathy," and "fellow-feeling" are the conceptual centerpieces of an eighteenth-century Scottish moral philosophy that consecrates the passions and thereby internalizes moral authority.

The romantic impulse would make its distinctly *religious* impression in the form of unpredictable "enthusiasm." As a relatively new theological phenomenon, enthusiasm became a cheeky eighteenth-century designation for erratic emotional displays believed to manifest heightened internal experience of the Holy Spirit. Field preaching was where this phenomenon appeared most regularly, and it was enthusiasm's repeated appearance at such gatherings that helped energize the pervasive spirit of revivalism defining the experiential undercurrent of eighteenth-century religiosity. That the theological roots of enthusiasm were of a pietistic genus further evinces the depth to which certain romantic impulses penetrated religious life. Pietism could serve as fertile soil for enthusiasm precisely because it had already become so thoroughly individualistic by midcentury; enthusiasm simply broke pietism free from its unspeakable Stoic heritage. If morals were reducible to the adjudication of passions, then it seemed more or less fitting that the experience of God could also be reduced to physically impassioned fervor. Kirk moderates were therefore justified in remaining suspicious over the deliberate stress upon internal experience of God's spirit, signaling as it did a severe and disturbing individualizing of genuine Christian faithfulness.[105] Enthusiasm attempted to do religiously what other romantic impulses attempted morally and politically: to rub smooth the social, liturgical, and teleological textures of worship and to absorb present feelings of natural experience. The unforeseen and perhaps most detrimental effect of enthusiasm would be its implicit marginalizing of both the moral and political integrity of religion itself.

Linking romanticism and its impulses to this book's central inquiry concerning a moral commercial order would overwhelm the reasonable limits of scope, so I will identify here only a few key connections. In some respects, romanticism corrects the abusive tendency of industrialization to ignore the agricultural foundation of political economy. Ironically, sacralizing nature aids in the erection of a protective barrier around its life-sustaining habitats. Observing custom offers a similar, more historically embedded means by which to impose defensive or prohibitory standards. Customs tell us about the past so that our present makes sense to us, securing stable continuity at the juncture of what was and now is. Customs do not reject newness or innovations out of hand; they simply discredit rapid or revolutionary novelties.

Conservative romanticism of the mid- to late-eighteenth century respected customs and the *telos* of nature they guarded. Radical romantics, on the other hand, sought to break the customary and teleological spine of commerce by asserting "rights" to two crucial political ideals: freer trade and social equality. The commercial sphere was believed to hold the keys for both modern portals. This brand of romanticism focuses more on the human experience of, and engagement with, nature than on nature itself. Broadly speaking, it is an ideology founded on ideal impulses. Freedom and equality are two such impulses, and to "realize" these ends the radical romantic proposes toppling the customs and institutions upon which political societies are founded and cultivated; that is, the romantic wishes to abolish all artifacts believed *un*natural to human self-expression. From the romantic starting point—the state of nature—human history is a dreadful story of how artifacts, especially commercial innovations, put further distance between human being and its natural home. Ferguson has shown us why this romantic insistence on overcoming artifacts is fictitious. History originates with artifact. Creation itself

---

105. For views of Kirk moderates on "enthusiasm," Ferguson included, see Richard Sher, *Church and University in the Scottish Enlightenment* (Princeton: Princeton University Press, 1985).

is an artifact, and necessarily political at that, due to the logical hierarchy of Creator over the created. Just as *in the beginning God created*, so too does humankind attempt to mimic genesis by making artifacts. History begins with creation and thus artifacts are part of history's beginning. Politically, God's providence includes institutions that safeguard lasting order: law, government, and economic exchange being but a few. The commercial order is an artifact that cannot be abolished, and even if abolished, its elimination cannot ensure either the ideal equality or freedom desired.

An excellent contemporary example of romantic temptations to unmake the political artifacts ordering civil society is that of economic deregulation. If government were to remove the entangling thicket of regulatory and legal measures meant to preserve a morally ordered marketplace—the assumption goes—then natural functions of the market when left to themselves would lead to the most efficient and profitable mode of human economy—the less involved is government, the more natural and virtuous the market mechanism. In the case of deregulation, the romantic impulse for freedom is clear: instincts and natural desires of the collective Will in commerce are such that acting on what is natural and allowing the market its natural course do the most good by affording the most public happiness. The true Romantic will thus reject the prospect of commerce in the sense of *commercium*—coming together—by definition. Genuine romanticism opposes true commerce simply by virtue of what it is.

CONCLUSION

Determinacy, universality, and romanticism have been referred to here as "themes," but could also have been described as "ideologies" or "theological perversions." Because Ferguson does not offer a positive or systematic moral or political theology I have portrayed him in an apologetic posture. Indeed, one may observe that it was in an age of overt theological austerity that the system we have come to call capitalism made its political genesis.[106] Or, to put it another way, only in the age of natural religion could an economic

---

106. This argument is one of comparison. Jonathan Edwards, George Turnbull, and perhaps Joseph Butler notwithstanding, eighteenth-century theologians are not reputed for their prowess. When compared to other periods of theological reflection, the qualitative contrasts become all the more striking. Thus, in suggesting that the eighteenth century is a period of "theological austerity," I mean only to say that the triumph of natural religion was in effect the crack in the political wall that when broken allowed for the impending surge of democratic capitalism. Theology that acknowledges only natural authority is a theology without fortitude.

system as morally unreliable as liberal democratic capitalism receive political sanction. In late-modern politics, moreover, not only do Western governments sanction capital markets, they positively *depend* upon them. Hamstrung by the shallowness of natural religion, moral and political reflection of the eighteenth century permitted the economy to take whatever structure or to continue whatever practice seemed most natural. And on this point the careful reader will have noticed how Ferguson's attention is drawn to the shadows and inconsistencies of the modern age. Determinacy, for example, is a pagan, not a Christian doctrine, and he rejects philosophers' attempts to draw upon "mechanistic" metaphors to shore up otherwise inept arguments about the natural world. "Mechanism" remains the standing metaphor for modern economics, and to the extent that the Market's natural functions are upheld as ultimately authoritative—as was the case in the eighteenth century—modern capitalism remains an ideological perversion of Christian metaphysics.

Universality is the eighteenth-century conversion of objective authority into subjective, a movement described by Hannah Arendt as "the dissolution of reality into subjective states of mind."[107] When authority becomes a thing to be *claimed*, as in the case of property, the totalization of rationalism is complete. This position of universality—the way the world exists being the way I see and believe the world to exist—frees the individual to pass judgment on any state of affairs so long as he is armed with ideals the judged-of can measure up to. Rational immediacy then leads naturally to an idealizing of moral and political realities, a digression from the concrete to the abstract. Rational immediacy means that whatever one thinks one knows to be the case simply *is* the case and no mediation is required. If total freedom and equality are rational possibilities for society, then it must also be a possibility in reality. Universality is the elevation of the human perspective to the point of ultimacy, and it was this subjective turn that also made determinacy and romanticism (ideally) possible.

Romanticism is dependent upon both the primacy of mechanical nature as well as a universalized human perspective because it is premised on the breakdown of any obstruction between the two ideals. As it has been addressed above, romanticism describes a series of *impulses*: appeals to a state of nature, sentimentalization of morals, and the emphasis on political novelty and rebellion. It first arises from the mythic state of nature, where the human being is wholly free of impediment, limitation, or customary artifact. The eighteenth-century hope is for communion with nature, or at least synchronization with nature's spirit. Newly achieved universality afforded romanticism an

---

107. Hannah Arendt, *The Human Condition* (Chicago: University of Chicago Press, 1998), 282.

opportunity to internalize (previously) metaphysical standards of action. The sentimentalization of morals is thus reflected overtly in the "moral sense," "sympathy," and "fellow-feeling" determining what ought to be done; what *ought* to be done is simply what the passions conditioned by nature determine of themselves. Rebellion against form is expressed most severely in violent revolution that seeks to lay waste to conventions and institutions bringing coherence to the fabric of society. The idea of "society" is itself an eighteenth-century obsession courting its fair share of admirers and despisers, but radical romantics are perhaps society's most indignant despisers of the period, and it is through them that the modern understanding of self-over-society in order eventually to be (partially) for society comes to life. Radical romantics search for pure expression of feeling in a state of nature. Feeling is a species of desire, and romantic desire reaches longingly for that natural object which raises desire to a higher plane of felicity—a desiring of desire. This eternally unsettled desire can find rest only in the Absolute, for, as Jean-Yves Lacoste has put it, "what excites our joy shows up our impotence to institute joy, to make it the perpetual tone of our experience."[108] Our relentless anxiety is evidence that desire cannot be fully realized and thus must be yet to come. "Beatitude," the fusion of heart and knowledge welded by vision of the Absolute, remains presently "restlessness," since "the heart wants what it cannot claim."[109] Ferguson for his part seems to have perceived the frontal edge of this crisis. The regularity with which he refers to the *Author* of nature is sufficient to highlight what he believes to disclose the depravity of a fictitious *state* of nature. The individualist energies of romanticism are crippled by the recognition that humanity is governed ultimately by an Author who is himself the subject of every heart's desiring.

Under the modern pressures of determinacy, universality, and romanticism, one begins to see the wisdom in Ferguson's concluding his *Essay on the History of Civil Society* with a treatment of political slavery. Each of these three themes undergirds modern democratic capitalism in the West, and it is truly astonishing that Ferguson had already detected many of its demented goals as early as the 1760s. The three political theologies he resists correspond to the threats modern capitalism imposes upon the meaning of history, human action, and political institutions. The latter three comprise the conceptual fortress within which societies thrive; the former three are the forces of capitalism rallying against the fortress gates. Political slavery is what occurs when walls

---

108. Jean-Yves Lacoste, "Le désir et l'inexigible: Pour lire Henri de Lubac," in *Le monde et l'absence d'oeuvre*, trans. Oliver O'Donovan (Paris: Presses Universitaires de France, 2001), 23–54.

109. Ibid., 53.

crumble and the fortress falls to capitalist siege. But this is as far as the martial metaphor can take us, for in actual fact the forces of modern commerce thus defined—determinacy, universality, and romanticism—are always already integrated into the life-blood of society itself. So understood, political slavery is the consequence of jettisoning distinctly *Christian* moral and political concepts informing modern society and adopting pagan or altogether unchristian ones. The descent into slavery is as rapid and thorough as the presumed escalation toward mastery. A morally corrupt society is susceptible to enslavement precisely because that society has undermined the fixtures making it "a society" as such. Determinacy, universality, and the romantic impulse are thus unmasked as ideals without substance, thrown into the light and exposed as "false spirits" actively destroying the very goods that pursuing them seemed to have promised.

2

The Meaning of History

What was history for the midcentury Scotsman? How did history present itself to the classically educated, religiously attuned, and politically savvy philosophers of the Scottish Enlightenment? Theorists were concerned both with what happened in the past, as well as how best to narrate what had happened in the past, differentiating closely between occurrences and interpretation of those occurrences. By attempting to take the Scottish questions as our own it will be useful first to identify why, exactly, history emerged from the shadows of natural philosophy when it did. Adam Ferguson was not the first to attempt retrieval of this semi-forgotten subject, and because he was not the first, retracing how the study of history was revived by the likes of Lord Kames, David Hume, William Robertson, and Adam Smith becomes all the more important. If Scottish thought of the period is concerned ultimately with the meaning of history and not merely its static factuality, then what might history mean for Adam Ferguson in particular?

In formulating a clear response to this question two underlying themes of Ferguson's philosophy of history will serve as guideposts for exploring more specific historical territories—Metaphysics and Institutions. Unconvinced as he was that the Newtonian portrait of a strictly law-governed universe offered the only truthful representation of the world, Ferguson did not abandon metaphysical thinking altogether for the simple reason that the study of history itself seemed to demand it of him. Metaphysical contours of history are defined by several acute polarities, or dialectics, that uncover the hidden meanings of history. In suggesting history has metaphysical shape we are reminded of characteristics not immediately perceptible or comprehensible; always pointing to something beyond itself. If history is at all metaphysical, then by definition it cannot be explained in *purely* physical terms; philosophical contemplation, not science, becomes the principal tool of historical investigation.

Once this brief sketch of history's metaphysical shape is complete, we may then turn to the concrete theme of Institutions. History cannot remain altogether abstract if it is to retain meaningful content. As a chronicle of what has happened in the world, it is vital that abstract metaphysical reflections map onto concrete political realities. Institutions are the flesh enlivened by a metaphysical soul legitimating history's mode of presentation to humankind. We shall want to resist the temptation merely to recollect and catalogue our modern institutions—a tedious and redundant method—and focus instead upon what institutions meant to our predecessors, what they mean to us, and what they might mean for generations to come. When can we be assured that some idea or event is truly meaningful? If the significance of institutions that either endure or disappear in history is established by their talent for disclosing meaning, then what is it about an institution that, as it were, changes things?

An institution's effecting change or being changed itself inaugurates an interruption of otherwise steady routines in worldly life. The question for most eighteenth-century historians was what advantages followed, or were implied by, these tectonic institutional shifts. On this point Ferguson takes bold departure from his fellow Scots: history is *not* the story of humanity's progress from savage to citizen; it is not inherently progressive and cannot establish contemporary superiority over the past. As becomes clear from his observations on the ancient Romans and North American "savage," history does not symbolize a series of interrelated narratives of an advancing or ever-improvable humanity. Ferguson's judicious treatment of history offers a richly textured hermeneutic that successfully accommodates certain types of progress and improvement but nevertheless rejects any declarations of superiority. Not even commerce, the Scottish school's dominant institutional force for progress, can explain the transitory character of politics and society. Commerce is but one institution among many.

Ferguson's critique of conjectural histories enlisting commerce as a primary catalyst for institutional progress comes in the way of defining the moral limits of economic exchange. Are there moral costs to the unyielding pressure for commercial gain? Is the good to be sought in interpersonal exchanges reducible to increased refinements and luxuries on the widest possible scale? Ferguson's exposition of history through the interpretive themes of Metaphysics and Institutions accentuates the mistake of viewing commerce as the vehicle of progress for political society. The *redemptive*, as opposed to conjectural, history of God's providence unmasks the myth of progress by revealing history's true Power. The meaning of history both emanates from and returns to God himself. To better understand how Ferguson made his way to this conclusion, we should now revisit the inner logic of these two themes and contrast them with views of his contemporaries.

SCOTTISH CONJECTURAL HISTORY

The staggering proportion of historical literature published by Ferguson's Scottish colleagues in the mid- to late-eighteenth century is nearly unparalleled in scale. David Hume, William Robertson, Lord Kames, and Adam Smith, to name only four, each produced reputable historical treatises of excruciating length and detail.[1] Their works differ from one another perhaps only in subject. But it is the scale, the overwhelming *quantity* of historical texts, that first attracts the reader's attention. The impressive number of monographs reveals intense fixation with the finer particulars of historic facts—scrutinizing every event and idea, arranging each factoid within a theoretically reconstructed state of affairs is much the methodological norm. But because the story of history was comprised essentially of facts, those facts could also be re-created in the present to communicate certain truths about the nature of human existence, especially man's capacity for making history itself. The more facts were collected, the fewer the errors or defects, the more pure and accurate the finished product. Scale came to symbolize extreme attentiveness and precision.

Facts of history narrate a story of progress when properly organized and outfitted to take their role in the plot of the historical saga. Dugald Stewart, the late contemporary of Scottish School historians and Adam Smith's biographer, felt proud enough with the ambitious achievements of these historians to ascribe their model the special status of "conjectural history."[2] The ideological background to this version of progressive history—a history signaling the perpetual improvement and advancement of humankind—was first inherited from Gershom Carmichael, the Scottish publicist of Samuel Pufendorf's *De*

1. David Hume, *History of England from the Invasion of Julius Caesar to the Revolution in 1688, Vols. 1-6* (Indianapolis: Liberty Fund, 1983); *Essays Moral, Political, and Literary*, ed. Eugene F. Miller (Indianapolis: Liberty Fund, 1987); Henry Home, Lord Kames, *Sketches of the History of Man, ed. James A. Harris* (Indianapolis: Liberty Fund, 2007); William Robertson, *History of Scotland, Vols. 1-2* (London: Routledge/Thoemmes, 1996); *History of America, Vols. 1-3* (London: Routledge/Thoemmes, 1996); Adam Smith, *The Wealth of Nations, Vols. 1-2*, ed. R. H. Campbell and A. S. Skinner (Indianapolis: Liberty Fund, 1981); *Lectures on Jurisprudence*, ed. R. L. Meek, D. D. Raphael, and P. G. Stein (Indianapolis: Liberty Fund, 1982).

2. Dugald Stewart, "Account of the Life and Writings of Adam Smith, LL.D.," in *Adam Smith: Essays on Philosophical Subjects*, ed. W. P. D. Wightman and J. C. Bryce (Oxford: Oxford University Press, 1980), 293.

Officio.[3] *De Officio* had made a case for the basic sociality of humankind and its subsequent progress through "four stages" of commercial advancement. This idea of irreducible sociality and its commercially driven progress proved enormously appealing to later Scottish historians.

Scottish reception of the four-stage theory was not unqualified, however. As Istvan Hont has explained, members of the Scottish school (especially Smith) were not aiming to redefine commercial society as such, but endeavoring "to integrate the fragmented aspects of Pufendorfian natural jurisprudence into a single theory of the history of civilization."[4] Theoretical foundations of a fundamentally commercial society were "already fully present" in Pufendorf's jurisprudence.[5] No, it was the *history* of this union between commerce and civilization that augmented Scottish imaginations. By redefining the history of society as essentially commercial, Pufendorf broke sharply from Grotius' theory of natural law, modifying it so drastically one could scarcely regard it as anything but an "invention."[6] Pufendorf's deliberate divergence from Grotian sociability to establish a commercially centered politics was, in fact, the real genesis of four-stage historiography.[7] Commerce was seen as the centripetal force of society and marketplaces the most public location for domestic trade, so empirical connections were ready to be drawn.

Distancing himself from Grotius still further, Pufendorf founded his theory of commercial sociability on private property. Interestingly, and again, entirely unlike Grotius, Pufendorf inserted his newly adopted authority of subjective rights directly into the historical storyline of property law.[8] The task of

---

3. Pufendorf served as professor of natural law at Heidelberg before relocating to Lund, where he held a professorship in the same subject and became the Swedish historiographer royal. He would later return to Germany and serve as Prussian court historian until his death in Berlin in 1694. See Samuel Pufendorf, *On the Duty of Man and Citizen*, trans. Michael Silverthorne, ed. James Tully (Cambridge: Cambridge University Press, 1991); *The Divine Feudal Law: Or, Covenants with Mankind, Represented*, trans. Theophilus Dorrington, ed. Simone Zurbruchen (Indianapolis: Liberty Fund, 2002); *Two Books of the Elements of Universal Jurisprudence*, trans. William Abbott Oldfather and Thomas Behme, ed. Thomas Behme (Indianapolis: Liberty Fund, 2009); *The history of popedom, containing the rise, progress, and decay thereof* (London: Printed for Joseph Hindmarsh, Royal Exchange, 1691); *The Law of Nature and of Nation* (London: Printed for J. and J. Bonwicke, R. Ware, J. and P. Knapton, S. Birt, T. Longman [and others], 1749). Gershom Carmichael, *Natural Rights on the Threshold of the Scottish Enlightenment*, ed. James Moore and Michael Silverthorne (Indianapolis: Liberty Fund, 2002).

4. Istvan Hont, "The Language of Sociability," in *Jealousy of Trade* (Cambridge, MA: Harvard University Press, 2005), 184.

5. Ibid.

6. Ibid., 164.

7. Ibid., 169.

justifying this argument for a subjective right to property would be carried out with the same careful analysis of history's movement toward "refinement and politeness" as helped support his original theory of commercial sociability.[9] Where Grotius had suggested social flourishing through "plainness" and "simplicity," Pufendorf introduced covetousness, ambition, and conflict. The four-stage theory was an essentially commercial vehicle turning on axes of property and refined progress. Nevertheless, this story could only be made coherent by relying upon the newfound instrument of subjective rights to secure peace, particularly those rights to private property and labor. The theory of basic sociality incorporated into rights-based natural jurisprudence hinged upon fluctuating and yet paradoxically stabilizing forces of economic necessity and want. Prolonged social solidarity became based on refinement's ability to further expand the marketplace. Thus, the history of society is the story of its commercial progress from property possession to the development of "great cities" where "the dynamics of progress become irreversible."[10]

The Scottish reception of Pufendorf's history of natural jurisprudence did not gain potency for several decades, however, until almost as a contagion the persuasive power of historical explanation came to its fullest life seemingly all at once in the thought of Hume, Robertson, Kames, and Smith. What interested these Scottish historians were history's causal connections to natural law and political society. They were concerned with the basic historical narrative of society and its institutions, but also with why society has a historical narrative in the first place and what kind of story history tells about it. Exploration of this deeper theme, the question of "why?," was pioneered most persuasively by Hume, who having accepted Pufendorf's theory of property in principle, sought then to redeploy it as a historical hermeneutic more to his liking.

For Hume, metaphysics is powerless to provide the analytical tools for serious historical research because of its tenuously unreliable and indefinite subject matter. No, the task of the historian is to identify and explain *laws* that would ultimately establish a science of man transcending metaphysics.[11] History is partly, if not predominately, defined by the relative transitions in this

8. Pufendorf's *On the Duty of Man and Citizen*. For a crucial essay challenging Richard Tuck on the idea of subjective rights in Grotius, and indeed the very idea of subjective rights, see Oliver O'Donovan, "The Justice of Assignment and Subjective Rights in Grotius," in *Bonds of Imperfection* (Grand Rapids: Eerdmans, 2004), 167–203. Greater attention to the political orientation of "right" will be given in chapter 4 of this thesis.

9. Ibid., 180.

10. Ibid., 183. Pufendorf's treatment of "great cities" is found in *Law of Nature*, 7.1.6.

11. David Hume, *A Treatise on Human Nature* (Oxford: Oxford University Press, 1978).

science of man from its earliest savagery to its latest commercial refinement. If the individual is a progressive being, then society experiences progress *de facto*. But getting this conjectural history off the ground requires at least one crucial assumption. As Christopher Berry has commented, "if human behaviour across space and time can be compared, if gaps can be plugged by conjecturing what may have happened, if it is feasible to write a history of mankind then there has to be a basic *fixity* or *constancy* in human nature."[12] Natural law governs reality by imposing specific limits on what presently occurs and on what will possibly occur in the future. The same can even be said, on Hume's view, for the natural law's arbitration of intellectual faculties. Every human mind is and must be uniform, for "the faculties of mind are supposed to be naturally alike in every individual."[13] Law demands the same predictable uniformity from the human mind as it does of reality itself:

> It is universally acknowledged that there is a great uniformity among the actions of men, in all nations and ages, and that human nature remains still the same, in its principles and operations. The same motives always produce the same actions: the same events follow from the same causes.[14]

Most of what one might conclude about the people of modern France or England, Hume claims confidently, could just as easily be concluded about the ancient Greek or Roman: "Mankind are so much the same, in all times and places, that history informs us of nothing new or strange in this particular."[15]

Nevertheless, despite overwhelming immutability, the fixity of human nature does not on Hume's account preclude the chance of long-term improvements. In addition to the Pufendorfian vision of commercial society historically conceived, an attitude of "optimism" had also pervaded the eighteenth-century consciousness. Leibniz's *Theodicy* is perhaps representative. In claiming that God could only have created the "best of all possible worlds," the aim to justify theologically the occurrence of every evil inadvertently induced (or at least encouraged) a spirit of rational optimism in early eighteenth-century political theorists.[16] Lord Shaftesbury and Alexander Pope

---

12. Christopher Berry, *The Social Theory of the Scottish Enlightenment* (Edinburgh: Edinburgh University Press, 1997), 68 (emphasis mine).

13. David Hume, *Enquiries Concerning Human Understanding* (Oxford: Clarendon, 1988), 80.

14. Ibid., 83.

15. Hume, *Enquiries*, 83.

inflect similar optimism in this regard, the latter going so far as to admit that in "spite of Pride, in erring Reason's spite, one truth is clear, *Whatever is, is Right.*"[17] Not many years later, eighteenth-century philosophers readily adopted the idea of intellect's immediate and untarnished interpretation of reality. Its tendency was to give itself over to additional optimisms. A perfectly created world governed by laws of a providential Deity implies that the mind's comprehension of reality is unlikely to be wrong and the authority of natural law unconditionally attributable to mind itself. It was this optimistic faith in the truthfulness of reality's presentation through the natural law and the certainty of mind to comprehend those presentations that spurned an inherently progressive history of society. Strangely, however, the notion that God's best possible creation could somehow be improved upon over time never struck the eighteenth-century mind as inconsistent. Part of what made this the best world was its openness to further improvement.

Hume's *History of England* was an attempt to reconstruct the facts of history to demonstrate just how far the English had truly advanced from its primitive, savage origins. Beginning with the ancient Roman settlements in Briton and concluding with the reign of William and Mary, Hume organizes what appears to be a historical outline framed by the cyclical loss and consecration of monarchs. Each volume, as it were, lifts the people of England onto higher planes and ushers them into grander vestibules. Approaching the seventeenth century and the conclusion of his historical journey, Hume highlights retrospectively the many sources of the kingdom's prosperity and pinpoints moments where this prosperity was needlessly curtailed. When liberty is promoted among a people—whether in commerce, policy, or literature—and interference from the monarch avoided, citizens are most happy and moral.[18] This explains why he concludes his treatment of the late-seventeenth-century monarchs with a summary of the period's "manners, arts, and science." When freedoms are allowed to run their course, their natural effect is social improvement in every category. A conclusion slow in completion, he wishes to show how society is *improved* when afforded political freedoms. The

16. On this point see Haydn Mason, "Optimism, Progress, and Philosophical History," in *The Cambridge History of Political Thought*, ed. M. Goldie and R. Wolker (Cambridge: Cambridge University Press, 2006), 195–217.

17. Alexander Pope, *Essay on Man* (Aldershot, UK: Scholar, 1988), emphasis mine.

18. "Governments too steady and uniform, as they are seldom free, so are they, in the judgment of some, attended with another sensible inconvenience: They abate the active powers of men; depress courage, invention, and genius; and produce a universal lethargy in the people" (*History of England, Vol. 6*, lxxi).

liberalization of trade and printed word simply bring the historical story to its eighteenth-century climax. The six volumes of the *History* were intended to remind Britons of their long-term progressive trajectory evinced in specific commercial and literary freedoms. A sequence of English monarchs structures the timeline of Hume's *History of England*, but this should not overshadow the real purpose of the regal lineup to demonstrate how monarchs infringe upon freedom and subsequently are forced to resign themselves to a "mixed" form of government.

Elsewhere, in "Of the Rise and Progress of the Arts and Sciences," Hume identifies four principles of artistic and scientific advance.[19] First, arts and sciences arise only where society enjoys free government. Expecting culture to blossom during the reign of an absolute monarch is "to expect a contradiction."[20] Second, and rather straightforwardly, nothing proves more favorable to rapid and prolonged political advantage than trading with like nations. One might recall it is from this principle that "jealousy of trade" is later brandished to justify self-perpetuating refinements generated by consistent international trade. The third and fourth principles support the claim that arts and sciences are best cultivated under different types of government, and that when any state reaches perfection it must from that moment naturally (and necessarily) decline.[21] Thus articulated, the hitherto implicit principles of Hume's *History* become firmly explicit: Progress is secured and energized by a free government with mixed constitution that encourages commercial refinement.

When one takes into account the totality of Hume's writings on the subject of trading liberties, one is inclined to interpret his insistence on the radical superiority of liberal government as being motivated fundamentally by the multiplied luxuries achieved in a free, unregulated commercial sphere. Indeed, he often seems to insist on liberal government for the *sake* of expanded freedoms in trade. But how then are we to respond to the last of Hume's principles: that when a state reaches perfection it must then begin to decline? One possibility might be to dismiss the principle as self-contradictory, a protective caveat to cover his flank from those mindful of ancient Rome. But Hume likely would have anticipated this objection, and in any event he appears actually to have in mind not the rise and fall of humanity in general, but of individual states. No state has ever reached constitutional perfection and there is no reason to

19. David Hume, *Essays Moral, Political, and Literary*, ed. Eugene F. Miller (Indianapolis: Liberty Fund, 1987), 111–37.

20. Ibid., 115, 117.

21. Ibid., 135.

believe one ever shall, but such challenges do not restrain human progress in arts and sciences over centuries. "The arts and sciences, like some plants, require fresh soil," and so even where one society may wither and decay another springs to life from its fertilization.[22] Hume's account of England's journey from ancient Roman territory to seventeenth-century dynasty is an account of how, exactly, progress happens materially. The meaning of history is what humanity can become if it establishes institutions conducive to the political and commercial liberties that promote luxury and refinement. He recites to us a story with several movements—from monarchical to mixed government, regulated trade to free trade, and even superstitious religion to natural religion—but regardless of which thematic variation one chooses, the Humean plot remains the same—progress is an intrinsic good to civil society.[23] Passage of time gives everyone a greater reason to hope.

Lord Kames and William Robertson took a similar view. Robertson's *History of America* and *History of Scotland*, following closely in the footsteps of Hume, arranges the histories of America and Scotland with the same agonizing detail and conjectural aspirations. Rehearsing these specific historical events should not confuse the fact, however, that all historical work no matter how detailed intends to make an *argument*; every historical event constitutes a premise reaching for a conclusion. For Robertson, each event and its unfolding consequences result from Divine providence and thus cannot possibly be accidental. The Almighty executes his purposes through perfect laws and gradually effects the kinds of change that gradually improve human affairs. "[S]acred history, by drawing aside that veil which covers the counsels of the Almighty, lays open his designs to the view of his creatures; and we can there trace the steps which he taketh towards them, with more certainty, and greater pleasure."[24] Historiography is the dominant mode of revelation.

Equally telling is the selection of Col. 1:26 for his sermon to the General Assembly—*Even the mystery, which hath been hid from ages and generations, but now is made manifest to his saints.* In his letter to the Colossians, Paul declares that the gospel of Jesus Christ was, until his bodily appearance, a hidden mystery. Robertson's reading of the text instead focuses on how society has progressed

22. Ibid., 137.

23. David Hume, *The Natural History of Religion* (London: A. and H. Bradlaugh Bonner, 1889). Polytheism gives way to a monotheism that will eventually give way to an even more "moderate" religiosity.

24. William Robertson, "A Sermon upon the Situation of the World at the Time of Christ's Appearance," *History of America, Book X* (London: Routledge/Thoemmes, 1996), 5–56. Sermon delivered in January 1755.

since the time of Christ and classifies several examples of contemporary superiority, including the abolition of slavery and establishment of just marital laws. He does not deny that Christ Jesus *is* the mystery St. Paul refers to in his letter to the Colossians; rather, his central point is that the revelation of Jesus Christ came at the most opportune time in history. The unfolding drama of God's providence *since* that revelation has taken the form of natural laws in the created order: "men came by degrees to understand this progressive plan of Providence, and to conceive how systems temporary and incomplete might serve to introduce that concluding and perfect revelation which would *declare the whole counsel of God to man.*"[25] History puts humanity in touch with conditions of ages past and thereby discloses gradual improvements to individuals and societies. "Mystery" has been gloriously revealed and *now* is the period of knowing. Importantly, our progress also includes "polished" morals to reinforce political institutions. By the hand of providence the present is made superior to the past and mankind fully comprehends this revealed fact since, as Robertson suggests, God has made his "whole counsel" known to him.

Lord Kames's *Sketches of the History of Man*, on the other hand, is a much more explicit reconstruction of history's progressive spirit. Kames felt that historiography had not gone quite far enough in its reformist program, as "there is still wanting a history of the species, in its progress from the savage state to its highest civilization and improvement."[26] Everything humans familiarize themselves with evinces marked advancement. Manners, commerce, government, law, reason, morality, and even theology are all naturally improved over time by man's increasing genius. God has endowed humanity with capacities for attaining higher and higher perfections with each passing age. When collected, the several smaller "sketches" of humanity's historical development unite to form a much grander portrait, wherein humanity is depicted in the most elegant and colorful light. If the portrait of humanity was once a primitive charcoal sketch, it is surely now an ornate masterpiece! Kames's *Sketches* is thus representative of a novel historical project of the Scottish school. No semblance of Ash Wednesday lingers—"from dust thou came and to dust thou shalt return"—but only ambition: "from dust thou came and to higher glory shalt thou ever go!"

Of all the representatives of the Scottish school, however, it was Adam Smith that made greatest use of Pufendorf's four-stage theory of history. The

---

25. Ibid., 10 (Acts 20:27).

26. Lord Kames, *Sketches of the History of Man*, ed. James A. Harris (Indianapolis: Liberty Fund, 2007), book 1.

four stages outlined in Smith's *Lectures on Jurisprudence*—Hunter, Shepherd, Agriculture, and Commerce—designate epochs, or constitutional transitions in the history of communities. His question concerns how contemporary society acquires a particular type of political order. Why, in other words, do we have *this* civil constitution rather than *that*? Smith's theory first emerges from an inquiry into the origins of government, where he outlines several different types of government found in the annals of history. Society began as a collection of hunters with no conception of private property and no institutions on which to found a government. When it was recognized that objects, particularly livestock, could be possessed personally, this recognition initiated the first constitutional transition from Hunter to Shepherd. From the Shepherd stage emerged the first semblances of monarchy, as one individual by virtue of capacity or resource became naturally acknowledged to lead and govern. Separating the Shepherd from the Agricultural stage is the notion of possessing territorial lands, whereby a mere chieftain soon becomes a consecrated monarch. On this configuration land is no longer common but seized and divided into tracts. Society takes the form of extreme hierarchy, control of the dispossessed is maintained by those who possess, and soil becomes the agricultural society's most precious commodity. The age of Commerce that emerges from the decay of Agriculture tends on Smith's account to begin with expanded domestic and international trade, but he had a difficult time explaining how, precisely, the transition from Agriculture to Commerce occurred as naturally as the previous two transitions. Unlike the first three stages, Commerce was not initiated by changing conceptions of property, and Smith likely conceived of Commerce following from Agriculture in much the way Hont has suggested, "in a purely quantitative sense" only.[27] Smith believed the Agricultural stage to be formally transcended. Interestingly, as was the case with Hume, this transition to Commerce would also naturally diminish the power of monarchical government and greatly strengthen republican sentiments. Even more interesting, though, is how the four-stage theory construes the establishment of constitutions. Smith's is a unique interpretation of history in that it gives *commerce* the power to break and refashion political structures. In the first two transitions this change is marked by revised conceptions of private property; in the latter two, labor is liberated from the necessity of the soil. Chieftain, monarch, and republic all emerge from revolutions in how basic commercial practices are understood within society. The power of commerce *precedes* the power of political institutions—commerce

27. Hont, *Jealousy of Trade*, 160.

is conferred a dangerously totalizing force within Smith's theory when the strength behind what society has become expresses its most basic object of pursuit.

Central to Smith's account, as it was for Robertson and Kames, is the conviction that each transition into a new constitutional epoch symbolizes divinely executed positive improvement. In part six of *The Theory of Moral Sentiments*, Smith claims:

> This universal benevolence, how noble and generous soever, can be the source of no solid happiness to any man who is not thoroughly convinced that all the inhabitants of the universe, the meanest as well as the greatest, are under the immediate care and protection of that great, benevolent, and all-wise Being, who directs all the movements of nature, and who is determined, by his own unalterable perfections, to maintain in it, at all times, the greatest possible quantity of happiness.[28]

God not only directs gradual improvements over time, but is also determined by his own inalterable perfections to provide creatures with the greatest possible quantity of happiness. Our Maker's universal benevolence is thus simultaneously progressive and felicitous. His mission in the world is to amend abject circumstances and strengthen feeble sentiments for the sole purpose of creaturely progress and enjoyment. The historian's task is to uncover exactly how this providence matures humankind and contributes to the happiness of commercial society. For Smith and his peers the many advances in science, art, literature, manners, and especially commerce answered the question of *how* each contributes to the architecture of gladness God establishes for his creatures. Freedom to enjoy the happiness derived from these provisions is all that is required, to allow the provisions to reach their appointed end.

It would be useful to restate the general principles underlying the conjectural model before turning our attention directly to Ferguson's more unusual hermeneutic. Conjectural history is first and foremost a fact-driven model. The task is to reconstruct facts of history with such precision and unremitting detail that the narrative builds incrementally to an apex where readers can behold the glorious heights to which humankind has ascended. The depiction was inherently and unreservedly progressive. Natural law, the

---

28. Adam Smith, *The Theory of Moral Sentiments*, ed. D. D. Raphael and A. L. Macfie (Indianapolis: Liberty Fund, 1982), VI.ii.3.1 (emphasis mine).

primary instrument of providence, could be discerned with immediate certainty and trusted to ensure uniformity in everyday experience. Indeed, for Hume this uniformity would extend even to individual members of society determined by law to live predictably ordinary lives. Perhaps more dominant than any other principle of the conjectural model, however, was the power of commerce to unite, inspire, and direct civil society and its institutions. In this sphere the hand of providence was most easily detected. The Scottish school's wooden, quasi-static version of providence tended to identify God's purposes either with what humankind would most like for God to accomplish or with what had transpired in past ages and was still sufficiently appreciated. It was, in other words, a selective providence twisted to serve humanity's moral improvement and maximal happiness.

Nearly unanimous in their acknowledgment of basic human progress, the notion became enshrined as a guiding light to historical interpretation. Material history, those past happenings that comprise specific facts of history, informs immaterial history, the ideas and meanings surrounding past happenings. Prioritizing material to immaterial history in this way inevitably suppresses the meaning of history latent in material facts: what happened in the past and what one presently thinks about the event are wholly correspondent, uniting the material "then" with the material "now." The preeminence of material history, however paradoxical, inaugurated the idea of intrinsic progress in history. In the hands of the Scottish school the need for historical respect was largely forgotten and then replaced by a story of relentless progress led chiefly by refinements in the commercial sphere.

ADAM FERGUSON ON HISTORY

Among the many eighteenth-century Scottish historical treatises, Adam Ferguson's are striking in their uniqueness and theoretical sophistication.[29] Here we have a theorist steeped in the classics, trained theologically for the Kirk, and who seems to prefer the ancient histories of moral and political thought to much contemporary commentary; a figure who (tellingly) conceives of philosophical inquiry as a *historical* investigation.[30] First evidence of his historical imagination arises early from a short pamphlet supporting stage plays, and can be traced

29. In making this claim I depart from those who include Ferguson in the Scottish conjectural school. See Lisa Hill, *The Passionate Society: The Social, Political and Moral Thought of Adam Ferguson* (Berlin and New York: Springer, 2006); H. M. Hopfl, "From Savage to Scotsman: Conjectural History in the Scottish Enlightenment," *The Journal of British Studies* 17, no. 2 (Spring 1978): 19–40; Christopher Berry, *Social Theory of the Scottish Enlightenment*, 70.

in greater maturity through his *Principles of Moral and Political Science*, *History of the Progress and Termination of the Roman Republic*, and *Essay on the History of Civil Society*. Ferguson's mind is always historically directed but maintains an alternative conception of history to that of his Scottish peers. David Allen summarizes the view well when he says, "the key appears to lie in Ferguson's preoccupation . . . with how the techniques required for studying past and present societies might be made to yield philosophical principles with far-reaching economic, political and ethical implications."[31]

But what conceptual distinctions set Ferguson apart? In responding to this question it would be useful to take up the generic themes proposed at the outset—Metaphysics and Institutions—and consider how they were deployed to address historical questions. In doing so it will become clear that Ferguson is not only disparaging of conjectural models of history, but aims also to purify the *methods* of historical inquiry. Using a variety of different illustrations and metaphors, from biological life-cycles to the fall of the Roman Empire, he permits the ideas and events of history to retain their complex integrity, interpreting them judiciously in their proper context and without forcing them into progressive molds. The circumstances from which ideas and events proceed are vital to how historical phenomena are correctly understood. History's logical movement is on his account neither conjectural nor cyclical, but a preliminary exploration of what can only be described as dialectical, a forerunner to a historical method later modified by Hegel and later German social theorists. In the course of our review of Ferguson's thought it will become increasingly apparent that he takes his greatest departure from the conjectural school on the question of commercial society. Conducting a history of commerce reveals that commercial force is only one of many powers forging constitutional changes in political society. The most decisive reason commerce cannot control narratives of progressive history, however, is because Divine providence, the true governing power of commerce, is neither unquestioning nor unselective. Providence makes *specific* provisions and is therefore misunderstood when construed as inherently progressive. Concepts of improvement and advancement are in themselves historically deficient and theologically vacuous. If God is ever concerned with improvement it is always first *redemptive*, for the idea of a God that improves without redeeming

---

30. Ferguson's library borrowing, for example, suggests a striking preference for classical literature over modern. See Jane Fagg, "Ferguson's Use of the Edinburgh Library: 1767-1806," in *Adam Ferguson: History, Progress and Human Nature*, ed. Vincenzo Merolle (London: Pickering & Chatto, 2008), 39–64.

31. David Allen, "Ferguson and Scottish History," in *Adam Ferguson: History, Progress and Human Nature*, ed. Vincenzo Merolle (London: Pickering & Chatto, 2008), 36.

substitutes the God who rights wrongs for a god content to promote felicities or refine manners. To understand how Ferguson conceives of the historical relation between providence and commerce, it is to the themes of Metaphysics and Institutions we should now turn.

Every philosophy of history implicitly or explicitly begins with a decision on method. The first question of *what* history is quickly morphs into a question of *how* history is. Ferguson's historical methodology is exploratory and sound, conversing interchangeably with rather disparate periods of history on their own terms. "The information they bring," he tells us, "is not like the light reflected in a mirror, which delineates the object from which it originally came; but, like rays that come broken and dispersed . . . only give the colours and features of the body from which they were last reflected."[32] He is critical of methodologies that appear to lean their conclusions too readily upon conjecture, and "to imagine that a mere negation of all our virtues is a sufficient description of man in his original state."[33] With statements like these, Ferguson is aware both of how notions of a "state of nature" are arrived at, as well as how Whig history is summoned to support this species of political inquiry. His contemporaries tended to view the past with present standards, imposing modern ideals of "manners" and "polish" upon supposed "barbarous" and "savage" nations of antiquity. The present is ill-qualified, however, "to prognosticate effects" or decide what should or should not have been the case in a past state of affairs. The present cannot discern with great specificity what societies of the distant past were like and thus "we can neither safely take, nor pretend to give, information on the subject."[34] We must insist upon a cautious reception. Comparing the present with the past qualitatively is not a valid moral or political methodology and does a great disservice to history itself. Ferguson understood that moral and political philosophy were interdependent fields of thought and that to locate answers to moral and political questions one would be required to travel easily between the two spheres. His methodology assumes that history is the place one goes for the wisdom to address compelling moral and political questions.

History remains an emphatically metaphysical subject in that it cannot reside exclusively in the material world but must also rely upon a variety of alternate powers for its continued existence, including memory, habit, communication, and place, all of which cooperate to support the life of history.

---

32. Adam Ferguson, *Essay on the History of Civil Society*, ed. F. Oz-Salzberger (Cambridge: Cambridge University Press, 1995), 76.

33. Ibid., 75.

34. Ibid., 76.

History becomes unintelligible when wholly naturalized because history is not explicable in purely natural terms. Intrinsic to history is a peculiar transcendence. The material historian might find it an easy task to tell us where and when the Act of Union was signed into law, for instance, but will find it woefully difficult to tell us *why* it was recommended or passed in the first place. History is as surprisingly elusive as it is decisive; which is another way of saying that it has both an abstract and concrete ontology. Ferguson perceived this tension and thus sought to reconcile the two polarities within a balanced historical inquiry, making each polarity central to the other for meaningful communication from past to present.

All history transpires in nature because humankind inhabits a natural world. What interests Ferguson, however, is how mankind *deals* with the world; not natural history *per se*, but mankind's nature historically conceived. In both *Principles* and *History*, he rejects any purported "state of nature" from which all humanity is a common descendant. He begins instead with the "order" of nature, which "consists of movements . . . [that] in a state of counteraction and apparent disturbance, mutually regulate and balance one another."[35] Never static or entirely uniform, nature contains within itself a principle of continual movement controlled by its own inner forces—an original movement is counteracted and a new movement begins afresh. Nature's ordered unity allows for societies to form and flourish by affording enough consistency for them to generate elaborate histories of their own. Any such history will offer two types of narratives: a "history of species" and a "history of mind."[36] The former narrative will inform the historian of the effects of mind, whereas the latter will inform him of the operations of mind itself. So, to gain the truest vision of humanity one must avail oneself both to the study of mind, as well as to its "varieties presented in the history of mankind."[37] To know what we are like we must examine what we have been like.

Ferguson wants to understand the meaning of mind's historical manifestations. Each such manifestation is unique and complex but never simply a production of human ingenuity. True ingenuity is attributable to the "wisdom of God," he explains, "not the deliberate effect of invention or choice."[38] One's earthly task is largely prescribed to them by their circumstance. Each person must vary his pursuits to match the exigency of the case. "The inventions of one age prepare a new situation for the age that succeeds; and

35. Ferguson, *Principles of Moral and Political Science* (New York: Garland, 1978), vol. I, 18.
36. Ibid., 49.
37. Ibid.
38. Ibid., 53.

as the scene is ever changing, the actors proceed to change their pursuits . . . [according] to the circumstances in which they are placed."[39] Man is meant to bend to reality, not reality to man, and thus reality's dominance defines for each person and society the terms of fruitful participation. Because humankind is shaped by reality it is thereby empowered to help shape reality itself. If there is anything ingenious about a human accomplishment it comes purely as a gift of God's benevolent wisdom. Nature and the human subject mutually accommodate one another according to the moving order established by Providence and its creative genius. Behind every good and truthful manifestation of mind is the wisdom of God giving or allowing it expression. Indeed, on this point Ferguson would have warmly affirmed the condemnation of natural religion issued by Friedrich Schleiermacher at the turn of the century: "Suavity and sociability, art and science have so fully taken possession of . . . minds, that no room remains for the holy Being that lies beyond the world."[40]

Nature is life-cycle consisting in ordered movements. The many parts of life come together in an unexpected unity established paradoxically by virtue of life's conflicting polarities: war and peace, freedom and determinacy, perfection and defect. What appears *prima facie* to be a profane conflict may regularly turn out to be the beginnings of peace; what was thought to be perfection was actually a defect; and so forth. Coherence is brought to these polarities by God's providential care. His order is evidence of a design that must be revealed to humankind, wherein "man is finally let into the *secret* of his own destination; and is enabled to become a conscious and willing *instrument* in the hand of his Maker for the completion of his work."[41] If, then, one is made aware of their destination, the task becomes one of discerning God's eternal will. Sometimes God's purposes are easily acted upon and sometimes they are not. This means the agent must consult the authority of history where the commands and wisdom of God consist in a living tradition. Sacred history discloses nature's deepest truth: that life comes from death, and that death, in turn, summons all created life: "While the things that were are passing away, things that were not are brought into being."[42] The moving life-cycle includes within itself the pinnacle of creation—humankind—whom God invites to look back upon the past from which it has come and glean the wisdom communicated.

This idea of "movement," and Ferguson's not-infrequent reference to "progress" or "progressive being," has persuaded many commentators to include

---

39. Ibid., 58.

40. Friedrich Schleiermacher, *On Religion*, trans. J. Oman (New York: Harper & Row, 1958), 1.

41. Ferguson, *Principles*, 166 (emphasis mine).

42. Ibid., 175.

him in the conjectural fold. Casting him in this way, isolating certain passages, fails to grasp the complexity of Ferguson's historical imagination. It is true that he characterizes man as an active, even progressive being, but this is primarily because man cannot possibly be stationary or static. Matter can appear stationary, of course, but human being is always "progressing," as it were, in a certain direction. Ferguson suggests, by and large, that though everyone tends toward progression of some form or other, the content of their progression will differ according to the object pursued: "Progressive natures are subject to vicissitudes of advancement and decline, but are not stationary, perhaps, in any period of their existence."[43] Human beings recognize within themselves a capacity for improvement motivated by a spirit of ambition to better themselves and their circumstance. At the same time, Ferguson also argues that profiting from these ambitious powers obliges one "to recollect what they are, and to take resolution respecting their purpose." His point, in short, is that progression should not be considered an open-ended horizon, but simply a natural process of human being directed toward a truthful end.

If it matters in what or how progress is made, or what kinds of progress are good or evil, then the *detection* of progress remains a crucial capacity in historiography. A striking difference arises between some particular innovation presenting itself and understanding the full significance or meaning of that innovation. The foremost difficulty, of course, is distinguishing a genuine innovation from false. Trajectories of persons or nations need time to develop and diffuse, and thus are often viewed in retrospect with many years separating the judge and the judged of. This distance yields a kind of intellectual humility, a patient suspension of judgment that permits the content of history to disclose itself on its own terms. There is no way of telling, really, in which general direction a person or society travels without some idea of their ultimate destination: "the sequel in the order of things is hid from our sight" and each is perfectly blind to future possibilities.[44] Speculating upon the future, particularly on the ultimate course of a given society, is like peering through the clouds and fog (James 4:13-17). On such evaluations science can teach us almost nothing, since there is little in "which the progress of mind is less questionable than it is in the attainment of science."[45] Although the ultimate goal of science is to explain reality and investigate its operations, it frequently disappoints by "pushing forward too fast" in hasty pursuit of discovery. If unchecked, this haste might also define judgments on the moral trajectory of an individual or society.

43. Ibid., 190.
44. Ibid., 315.
45. Ibid., 271.

It is better, thinks Ferguson, to take the long view—to step back and define the wider contours of civil society's topography.

Returning to the notion of life-cycle and nature's movement through contrasting polarities, it is notable that Ferguson uses the development of memories and habits to transition from a mostly personal interrogation of progress, to a dynamically social one. Memories and habits are personal, yes, but they are also corporate, and each requires time to gain its communicative momentum. Ferguson narrows his attention to the impact of habits on political constitutions, and in particular their propensity for stimulating intellectual prejudices, since "the authority of government itself, under every political establishment, rests on the habits of thinking which prevail among the people."[46] He captures here an element of truth in popular sovereignty: sometimes habits are for the best politically and sometimes they are for the worst, but in either case habits are essential to the enduring stability of civic order. Habit expresses itself politically through customs. As a history of action, habits serve as channels down which the current of human morality travels. Habits of thought and action determine together the directional character of civil society. Society utilizes habits to balance the life-cycle's repetitive clash of polarities and drive them onward in one contiguous direction. Improvement is one natural end for society, decline the other. But it should be remembered that the question before us is metaphysical and asks specifically *why* progress or decline comes about when it does. What criteria are observed when making judgments of this kind? History is a narrative of past transactions, to be sure, but does it then follow that the plot of this narrative is contrived? Not obviously. A principle of progress in human nature might elicit one's longing for improvement, but gratifying this desire is never guaranteed, and even if granted rarely takes an anticipated form. Progress is therefore an object of human longing that extends always beyond human control.

Here the metaphysical character of Ferguson's historical thought becomes strikingly less opaque. "The material world was made . . . not for itself, but for the mutual communication of minds and forming a system of signs and expressions in which the infinite author makes himself known to his intelligent creatures."[47] As a means of Divine communication, man's task is to participate with God in the world's redemption. Indeed, "the first object of concert or convention on the part of man is not to give society existence" or attempt novelty in a world already created, "but to perfect [the] society in which he finds himself already by nature placed."[48] Humanity is responsible for assisting

46. Ibid., 215.
47. *Principles*, 272.

God in his redemptive purposes without being motivated by reward, since "every step and every movement of the multitude, even in what are termed enlightened ages, are made with equal blindness to the future."[49] Therefore, one may conclude that the best one can do is

> view himself as but part in the community of living natures; by which he is in some measure let into the design of God, to combine all the parts together for the common benefit of all; and can state himself as a willing instrument for this purpose, in what depends on his own will; and as a conscious instrument, at the disposal of providence, in matters which are out of his power.[50]

Having shown that the general direction of society cannot be known, much less shouted from the rooftops, Ferguson suggests that movements of society, like everyday movements of individuals, take one faint step at a time. The history of species is the story of society's advancement and decline, improvement and corruption; a history of mortals that carries the fascination of historians only so far. The history of mind, on the other hand, allows for much more interesting metaphysical speculations. On this subject he distinguishes strictly between the material and the immaterial:

> There are limits set to the progress of [man's] animal frame. It is stationary; it declines; and is dissolved: but to this progress of intelligence, in ascending the scale of knowledge and of wisdom, there are not any physical limits, short of the universe itself, which the happy mind aspires to know, and to the order of which he would conform his will.[51]

In the section "Of the Future State" which concludes the first volume of the *Principles*, Ferguson argues further that although the material of humanity has an unthinkable future, "it is no violent stretch of imagination to conceive the human soul, in its present state, as the embryo of a celestial spirit."[52] Mankind is intended to participate in God's redemptive purposes on earth so that it may

48. Ibid., 262.
49. *Essay*, 119.
50. *Principles*, 313.
51. Ibid., 331.
52. Ibid., 330.

participate eternally in his life after work on earth is done. The highest calling is to participate with him so as to forever live in him. Mind is that immaterial part of man which, after bodily death, becomes the everlasting company of God. Eternality unlocks mind's potential and renders it actual.

These broadly metaphysical concerns highlight Ferguson's objection to historiographies that presume to judge conclusively on the moral orientation and political trajectory of society. Methodologically this meant treating the subjects of historical inquiry with caution and dignity, allowing them to communicate their own questions from their own unique context. The present is not superior to the past by virtue of its convenient existence at a later point in time. Some conclusions can be drawn by observing the historical development of a given society; some cannot. What surely cannot be judged with sufficient accuracy is whether a people progress toward greater and greater refinements; whether, in other words, one society can ever be rightly considered superior to another. Ferguson's argument has been that a society's true character is transcendent in that its moral direction can never be self-determined or self-assigned. Scientific discovery, despite its promises and noble aspirations, cannot reduce, test, dilute, or otherwise explain the problem away. No amount of observation or experimentation will abolish the transcendent beauty of the world. What often appears progressive—like the caterpillar's maturity to butterfly, or the merchant's continued acquisition of wealth—may prove in the end merely to have initiated the beginnings of ruin. If societies experience progress or decline it must be determined what *kind* of progress or decline is being experienced or sought. And in drawing this distinction, the distinction of kind, we approach the second theme of Ferguson's philosophy of history, Institutions.

Historically speaking, how do institutions form a narrative that clarifies the ambiguities of politics? Do institutions possess a greater descriptive power that nature can only point toward indirectly? For Ferguson the answer to this latter question clearly is "yes," and the task of outlining this theme will be to respond to the question of why institutions receive and contribute unique historical meanings. Methods seeking only to describe persons, places, ideas, events, or institutions of history are bound to disappoint, as such descriptive efforts are usually as tedious as they are uninteresting. History is shaped by the ever-changing harmony of these forces, each striking its own note and inspiring the historian in a different way. Hume was correct to suggest that history contains certain seamless regularities and constancies, but was wrong to insist that such fixity determines how history should be interpreted. The song that history sings may retain its basic form, indeed it must, but the many different sopranos, tenors, and basses uniting to vocalize the harmony of history's song are often wildly unpredictable. Without doubt the most moving moments of any choral arrangement are those that shatter expectations! Meaning emerges from history as moments of surprise, spontaneity, or intense breakthrough. That Bach expresses a tendency to appreciate certain notes or harmonies and uses them with frequency is easily overshadowed by the dazzling originality of his artistic expressions. History, too, expresses certain uniformities, as Hume suggests, but its regularities and constancies become meaningful only when interrupted or transformed. Institutions serve as anchors of history in much the same way C-minor occupies Bach's Cantatas; the fixity of institutions provides a gravity regulating the unpredictable force of ideas and events. Institutions become, as it were, the historian's starting point.

But what *is* an institution? Initially the term's use was theological and referred to a contiguous authority established by God to direct and order human affairs. Marriage, law, church, university, all represent institutions divinely imputed and governed. They are chiefly inherited, not assigned; their authority and continued legitimacy is vouchsafed by God and assisted by public faith, habits, and prejudices. Human beings are born into particular places at particular times, and institutions furnish the authoritative boundaries for human action in political life. Institutions are involuntary in the sense that they are not presented to the public as a collection of equal options from which to choose. And yet, for Ferguson, although a society's inherited institutions continually exert enormous force on social consciousness, each relies tenuously upon sustained public honoring of that force. In fact, authority of government itself "rests on the habits of thinking which prevail among the people."[53] The actual *thinking* of a people about their institutions contributes directly to the ever-fluctuating influence and durability of the institutions themselves. Questions of how institutions are experienced, therefore, logically precede their later formation *of* human experience.

Upon institutions "civilization" is founded.[54] For Scottish school historians this title of "civilization" was awarded, in addition to their own, only to the ancient Greek and Roman states. On their view these "masculine" yet vanquished republics represent the origin of a progress that European societies have since been avidly seeking to replicate. Both Hume and Robertson began their histories of England and Scotland at their ancient roots. Ferguson, on the other hand, takes the question of institutional progression from a different angle and draws notably different conclusions. His moral and political thought

53. Ibid., 215.
54. Ibid., 252.

remains institutionally, as opposed to socially or conventionally centered, because society and conventions revolve around institutions much like planets do the sun, receiving energy from their furnishings and providing equilibrium to everyday life.

In his *History of the Progress and Termination of the Roman Republic*, Ferguson illustrates how institutions might be historically conceived. As the title indicates, the book narrates constitutional alterations of ancient Rome from their republican beginnings to their despotic end. His method imitates in many ways the descriptive style of Robertson and Hume, but does so under radically different assumptions of what that history ultimately means. In his erudite article on political "threats" in Ferguson's *Roman Republic*, Iain McDaniel explains that "Ferguson's insistence upon the relevance of classical history for a proper understanding of modern Europe's political trajectory sets him at some distance from other Scottish Enlightenment thinkers," who "generally emphasized the superiority of modern commercial societies over their ancient more 'barbarous' predecessors."[55] Roman history meant something to contemporary Europe because the story of Rome mapped nicely onto modern political affairs. The issues that either plagued or benefited Rome seemed also to plague or benefit modern Europe, suggesting that many moral and political questions always remain perennial. Montesquieu had made a similar claim only a few decades prior, and from him Ferguson inherits the interpretation of Roman decline as a consequence of "corrupted public spirit" attending constitutional transitions toward democratic sovereignty.[56] Disagreement between the two theorists is visible too, of course, but essential for our purposes is what Ferguson's understanding of ancient Roman institutions tells us about his philosophy of history. His point seems to be that "progresses" assigned to civilizations of modern Europe could also be assigned to ancient Rome. Rome is not merely a society from which modern society has arisen and upon which it frowns; rather, it is a society with abundant political analogues that would, if consulted, impart wisdom to cope with similar questions. In Rome's case the obsessive pursuit of greater territories and pleasures slowly destabilized institutions preserving social cohesion and anesthetized public spirit. But Ferguson nowhere argues that these corruptions

---

55. Iain McDaniel, "Ferguson, Roman History and the Threat of Military Government in Modern Europe," in *Adam Ferguson: History, Progress and Human Nature*, ed. Vincenzo Merolle (London: Pickering & Chatto, 2008), 116.

56. Montesquieu, *Considerations on the Greatness of the Romans and Their Decline*, trans. David Lowenthal (New York: Free Press, 1965). Ferguson's reading of Montesquieu, as will be seen more clearly later, is most pronounced in latter sections of his *Essay*.

ultimately converted Rome from a republican to monarchical constitution. The problem was much more complex than that. Instead his modest argument is that modern European nations, like ancient Rome, are susceptible to capricious swings between popular and monarchical tyranny. The *real* political problem is anarchy. Ancient Rome had lost the power of its institutions because their authority was undermined, becoming

> by degrees, and at every succession, more and more mercenary or venal in the choice of their masters, more brutal in the exercise of their force against fellow-subjects, and, with a continual degradation from bad to worse, substituted order, courage, and discipline of Roman legions, [for] mere ferocity, with a disposition to mutiny as well as rapine.[57]

The empire appeared healthy at its outer extremities while secretly rotting in its center. It subsequently underwent two ideological transitions, one moral and one political: from republic to monarchy, and from Epicurean to Stoic convictions. We are concerned here only with the latter transition, from Epicurean to Stoic. When there were rights to preserve and public duties to perform, the Roman people were persuaded to align themselves with Epicurus and establish pleasure as the highest standard of good and evil. But when public occupations were taken from them and their personal safety jeopardized they quickly returned to the idea that "men were made happy by the qualities which they themselves possessed, and by the good they performed, not by mere gifts of fortune."[58] Romans turned their hearts from Epicurus to Zeno for consolation.

In this way, therefore, philosophical ideas—their usual commitments included—are seen to emanate from political circumstances, not vice versa. Political and moral convictions were deeply intertwined: the empire grew, commerce flourished, and the land was cultivated, "but these were but poor compensations for the want of that rigor, elevation, and freedom of mind, which perished with the Roman republic itself, or with the political character of the other nations which had been absorbed in the depths of this ruinous abyss."[59] Institutions had endured gradual, almost imperceptible deterioration at the hand

---

57. Adam Ferguson, *The History of the Progress and Termination of the Roman Republic* (Edinburgh: Bell & Bradfute: 1825), 391.

58. Ibid., 394.

59. Ibid., 396.

of the very people these institutions supported, and thus ancient Rome collapsed under the weight of its own decadence.

The story of ancient Rome illustrates how and why institutions are initiated, changed, protected, or abolished. Every new variation is a budding flower ripe with meaning. Ferguson's investigation of the "Savage" and "Barbarian," the historic creatures so disparaged by Scottish school historians, reinforces this point. In early sections of the *Essay*, Ferguson isolates the question of what man's exertive actions can actually accomplish. The best historical method takes "the history of active Being from his conduct in the situation to which he is formed, not from his appearance in any forced or uncommon condition."[60] The Savage and Barbarian, for example, should be treated contextually as a product of their placement. Notions of a progress from animal to citizen are nothing but presumptuous fantasies and inventions. If it is admitted that man possesses a principle of improvement, then that improvement has only to do with what he is capable of achieving, and nothing more. All the latest efforts at newness and advantage are but a continuation of past endeavors, and whether or not one naturally advances toward or retreats from noticeable improvement remains mostly concealed. Determining what is truly "natural" about progress always proves treacherous because of the term's unavoidable ambiguity, and because "the actions of men are equally the result of their natures."[61]

The savage in Ferguson's *Essay* is represented by the "Indian" of North America, who pays little attention to property, lives mostly for subsistence, views his habitation pragmatically, and lives equitably with peers. There exists little sign of subordination and each member is content to live according to the natural furnishings of nature. For savages, "power is no more than the natural ascendancy of mind; the discharge of office no more than a natural exercise of the personal character, and while the community acts with an appearance of order, there is no sense of disparity in the breast of any of its members."[62] The bonds that bring savages together are those of genuine affection and friendship. Property is unthought-of because it is not yet viewed as a requirement for life. "No man is naturally indebted to another" and therefore the community is free of unequal treatment. It is only when friendship becomes defined in terms of duties or favors that the bonds of friendship are corroded, as the importation of obligations into the frame of relations eliminates its friendliness. The presumption of equality is abolished by a sense of indebtedness, giving

60. Ferguson, *Essay*, 9.

61. Ibid., 15.

62. Ibid., 84.

one member of the community leverage over another. Trust is lost; suspicion prevails. But the Savage avoids this problem by seeing justice as a matter of *fitness*, "not the distinctions of equipage and fortune."[63] To illustrate this conceptual difference: "in Europe to fall in battle is accounted an honor; among the [savages] it is reckoned disgraceful."[64] They are a capable people without (European) ambition. Ferguson is persuaded that once the savage has taken note of dangers that commercial arts admit, he loses the freedom that only his native culture naturally endows—"however tempted to mix with polished nations, and to better his fortune, the first moment of liberty brings him back to the woods again; he droops and he pines in the streets of the populous city."[65] Commercial gain is for the savage a small temptation, but one quick to atrophy with the deadening of competitive energy.

What differentiates the Savage from the Barbarian is the latter's recognition that property can be privately possessed. For the Barbarian, the "common" is already a *divided* common.[66] A specific application of labor to a specific place "aims at an exclusive possession," and "when the individual no longer finds among his associates the same inclination to commit every subject to public use, he is seized for his personal fortune; and is alarmed by the cares which every person entertains for himself."[67] Thus it is only when others are known to be withholding from the public and hoarding out of fear of not-having that one seeks to acquire what best supports subsistence. Herds are the initial source of the Barbarian's wealth. Each occupies himself with his own doings, his own accumulation, and his own advantage. And yet, explains Ferguson, one "may now apprehend, that the individual having now found a separate interest, the bands of society must become less firm, and domestic disorders more frequent."[68] Unequal distribution of property introduces a permanent subordination resulting in total abolition of equality. Property first initiates and then encourages competition, strife, and violent conflict. Unity is forged anew only by allegiance to a leader recognized for their amassed fortunes. Thus, in the society of Barbarians, fortune replaces capacity, generosity, and friendship: "Every nation is a band of robbers, who prey without restraint, or remorse, on their neighbors."[69]

63. Ibid., 88.
64. Ibid., 91.
65. Ibid., 94.
66. On this point Ferguson departs clearly from Locke.
67. Ibid., 95.
68. Ibid., 97.
69. Ibid.

Ferguson agrees with Scottish peers that recognition of a "fortunate" leader is the beginning of monarchical government, but disagrees with where this logic leads historical thinking. When the Chieftain or King becomes "the object of veneration" he also becomes the highest object of national unity, their "common bond of connection."[70] Upon coronation the monarch seeks to expand his dominion by conquest, which serves to further unite the nation against a common enemy and doubly reinforce allegiance to the king. The Barbarian is reduced to a useful instrument, for "when interest prevails in every breast, the sovereign and his party cannot escape the infection . . . to turn his people into property, and to command their possessions for his profit or his pleasure."[71] This is what happens, thinks Ferguson, when interest rather than laws guides a sovereign and his people; the logic of acquisition halts not even at the insidious possession of people. Mankind is everywhere divided, and interest drives the wedge still deeper.

Stepping back from our direct investigation of the Savage and Barbarian, in what way are they practically serviceable to Ferguson's philosophy of history? As with the narrative of the Roman Empire, it seems that the Savage and Barbarian are intended to illustrate the incoherence of reading progress into the institutional plot of history. The supposed "rude" nations of the past (a term Ferguson identifies with "disorder") are *not* to be considered as inferior to our own:

> We are generally at a loss to conceive how mankind can subsist under customs and manners extremely different from our own; and we are apt to exaggerate the misery of barbarous times by an imagination of what we ourselves should suffer in a situation to which we are not accustomed. But every age hath its consolations, as well as its sufferings.[72]

Projecting oneself and one's circumstance onto history is a tempting fallacy for even the most cautious historian, but history must not be considered as an account of how institutions of the present came to ascendancy over institutions of the past. The rise and fall of the Roman Empire and the basic political

---

70. Ibid., 99. It is worth noting at this juncture the similarity between the language used here by Ferguson to refer to the "bonds" of union in societies and the political language of Augustine in *City of God*. The correspondence is not likely accidental.

71. Ibid., 101.

72. Ibid., 103 (emphasis mine).

configuration of Savage and Barbarian societies are analogues to the truth that institutions, like the people they govern, are susceptible to transforming movements. Rome seemed to be progressing just fine until it unexpectedly collapsed; the Savage seemed (on Hume's and Robertson's accounts, anyway) to show signs of rudeness and depravity when in fact he was happily content with primitive subsistence. On both accounts Ferguson shows that institutions are not self-directed toward political perfection. Any discernible difference between the ancient and modern—between "rude" and "polished"—is purely a difference of kind and not of worth. His treatment of the Roman and Savage demonstrates that institutional changes prompted by commercial forces within these rude societies, though such forces may appear to modern eyes intrinsically conducive to political improvement, were for these societies corrosive to the affective powers that held them together. There is little reason to view the ancients as less polished or civilized: "they have merited and obtained our praise" by "their penetration, the ability of their conduct, and the force of their spirit."[73]

A natural law of progress cannot long exist because, as Prof. Collingwood has nicely put it, the idea of a law of progress, "by which the course of history is so governed that successive forms of human activity exhibit each an improvement on the last, is . . . a mere *confusion of thought*, bred of an unnatural union between man's belief in his own superiority to nature and his belief that his is nothing more than a part of nature."[74] Similarly persuaded, Ferguson suggests societies are largely a product of their place and circumstance, and any advancement or improvement considered only *in kind*. Commerce is conspicuously referred to as a category of "art," prescribed to humanity by its place, controlling to some degree what can or cannot be contributed. In a period of conflict the energy of arts will be comparatively low as national felicity is doused by the burden of war. The artistic is latent in every human soul and only requires favorable circumstances to draw it into the open. Modern Europe is artistically indebted to the ancients only to a small degree, since they provided merely the "materials" and "form" of artistry and not the felicitous motivation. Arts arise spontaneously from the human mind wherever men are cheerfully placed. And yet, in a statement strangely resonant with Heidegger's "The Origin of the Work of Art," "it is difficult to find the origin of any art."[75] The steps toward perfect art are numerous and "we are at a loss on whom to bestow the greatest share of our praise; on the first, or on the last, who may have borne a part in the progress."[76] Commercial arts, a class of

---

73. Ibid., 189.

74. R. G. Collingwood, *The Idea of History* (Oxford: Oxford University Press, 1994), 323 (emphasis mine).

artistic activity, arise from affections and, like literary arts, are "promoted by circumstances that suffer the mind to enjoy itself."[77] Art offers something new to civilization conditionally, and the perennial question remains whether this newness constitutes a genuine *improvement*.

Does the process of the old giving way to new imply superiority? From whose point of view could such a judgment be determined? Here again Collingwood is insightful. The problem with latent progress is that experience shows us that the new generation has a difficult time entering sympathetically into the life of the old—the new generation "sees life as a mere incomprehensible spectacle, and seems driven to escape from sympathy . . . by a kind of instinctive effort to free itself from parental influences and bring about the change on which it is blindly resolved."[78] It is precisely because of this inability to sympathize that

> the historical changes in a society's way of life are very rarely conceived as progressive even by the generation that makes them. It makes them in obedience to a blind impulse to destroy what it does not comprehend, as bad, and substitute something else as good. But progress is not the replacement of bad by the good, but of the good by the *better*.[79]

Art *develops* but cannot be said to progress. And as commercial arts cooperate with institutions it becomes clear, on Ferguson's account, that art leaves a historical impression on institutions that may not turn out to be an improvement at all. Political institutions are initiated and concluded, contracted and expanded, altered and preserved; they are both a product of, and force upon, civil society. Against the Scottish school therefore Ferguson argues that commerce does not always administer improvements but may also degenerate and corrupt even the most cultivated bonds of cohesion.

The two generic themes we have considered in Ferguson's historical thought—Metaphysics and Institutions—appear on closer examination to take

---

75. Ibid., 163. See Martin Heidegger, "The Origin of the Work of Art," in *Basic Writings*, ed. David Farrell Krell (San Francisco: HarperCollins, 1993), 139–204. *"The origin of the work of art—that is, the origin of both the creators and the preservers, which is to say of a people's historical existence—is art."*

76. Ibid.

77. Ibid., 165.

78. Collingwood, *Idea of History*, 326.

79. Ibid. Collingwood is not advocating progress, of course, but rather outlining its logical contours.

on a sharply *dialectical* character. History widens prudence by stretching and informing it of customs and conventions corresponding to present reality. Ferguson's historical writing, as David Kettler explains, "embodies a method, but does not pronounce on method," allowing him to "hold alternative possibilities in suspension, while moving to a conclusion and achieving an effect at a level different from that upon which the possibilities clash."[80] Hume, of course, is known to have disliked the *Essay* so much as to discourage Ferguson from going ahead with publication, and although Hume's letters on the subject are unclear as to why he thought so, the tone with which his disagreement is expressed draws further contrast between the preferred methods of each historian. Moreover, as Italian historian Vincenzo Merolle urges, "Hume is a man of the Enlightenment, Ferguson a precursor of Historicism and Romanticism."[81] The ideas and method of the *Essay* belong more to the nineteenth than to the eighteenth century. Ferguson could identify the faulty logic of historical progress while simultaneously acknowledging the historical fact that life changes—his method allows for this tension. A primitive brand of historicism was introduced that even his contemporaries could identify as original. The "secret substratum of the *Essay* was not the philosophy of the Enlightenment but a philosophy that sought . . . to comprehend theory as a historical practice—historicism."[82]

This helps explain Ferguson's taking a historical view of morality and politics and why his philosophy of history appears proto-Hegelian. Ferguson's position toward history manifests itself throughout the corpus of his work—moral and political philosophy are joint *historical* explorations. In the *Principles*, but even more explicitly in the *Essay*, he employs an unrefined dialectical method that hangs together precisely as Kettler has suggested, in suspension. Affirmation is often followed by denial; freedom is pitted against determinacy; life gives itself to death and death gives itself to life. History progresses and declines and its dialectic movement gathers still greater exploratory momentum through successive human experiences.

The rough-edged historicism and primitive dialectic in Ferguson's thought are also confirmed by the German reception of his historical works in the late eighteenth century.[83] It is difficult to say with any exactness what Hegel himself thought of Ferguson's historical method, but clearly "Ferguson's complex view

80. David Kettler, "History and Theory in Ferguson's 'Essay on the History of Civil Society': A Reconsideration," *Political Theory* 5, no. 4 (November 1977), 437–60.

81. Vincenzo Merolle, "Hume as a Critic of Ferguson's *Essay*," in *Adam Ferguson: Philosophy, Politics and Society*, ed. Vincenzo Merolle (London: Pickering & Chatto, 2008), 73–87.

82. Ibid., 84. Merolle refers here to Baron D'Holbach.

of history, allowing patterns of progress and regress and tying them to deliberate human actions, fascinated and baffled" his German counterparts.[84] The best we can do is infer from a comparison of Ferguson and Hegel's historical methods notable similarities suggesting a common historical outlook. Disincluded from this list of similarities, obviously, is the idea of historical progress—a view Hegel endorses with confidence and Ferguson largely rejects.

Describing Ferguson's historical method as dialectical returns us to the analogy of the life-cycle referred to above. Conjectural history is expressly premised on the idea that history naturally progresses. Its unspoken premise, however, is the idea that *nature itself* progresses. This latter premise was made possible by conceptual transitions several decades earlier when matter, the stuff of the universe, became "the quantitatively organized totality of moving things."[85] For the ancient Greeks, on the other hand, there was no "dead" matter: "nature was a vast living organism, consisting of a material body spread out in space and permeated by movements in time; the whole body was endowed with life, so that all its movements were vital movements; and all these movements were purposive, directed by intellect."[86] Unlike the ancients, late-renaissance theorists perceived reality as a multiplicity of united objects absent of imposed form. Mind and the material world were fused. Ferguson is clearly most sympathetic with the ancient view of nature.[87] In a short section

---

83. Two of the better texts exploring this link are Fania Oz-Salzberger, *Translating the Enlightenment* (Oxford: Clarendon, 1995), and Norbert Waszek, *The Scottish Enlightenment and Hegel's Account of "Civil Society"* (London: Kluwer Academic, 1988).

84. Oz-Salzberger, *Translating the Enlightenment*, 316.

85. R. G. Collingwood, *The Idea of Nature* (Oxford: Clarendon, 1945), 112.

86. Ibid., 111.

87. Others have agreed. The German historian Reinhart Koselleck has suggested that the concept of progress is itself modern in origin and could not have emerged prior to the eighteenth century, lending support to the reconceptualization of history into a justification of the future. He thinks "it may be indisputably presupposed that progress is a concept specifically calibrated to cope with modern experiences, namely that traditional experiences are surpassed by new ones with astonishing speed." This acceleration of human experience at the hands of progress has forced three uniquely modern steps: universalization of progress's subject (applying to all spheres), embodiment of progress as a historical agent, and consecration of progress as its own subject. In contrast to progress, any "decay" wrought by this misstep is simply incorporated back into the progressive process as natural fertilizer to its continued growth. And yet, "precisely because and so long as progress is unfinished, the chances of decay increase—admittedly, no longer read in natural metaphorics but rather in the sense of catastrophes that human beings have become capable of bringing about for themselves with the technological powers at their disposal." Progress thus makes plans while at the same time redefining the goals these plans shoot for. Moderns strive for a progressive horizon that is actually an abyss. See "'Progress' and 'Decline,'" in *The Practice of Conceptual History*, trans. Todd Presner (Stanford: Stanford University Press, 2002), 224.

of the *Principles* ("The Origin of Evil") he claims that "the whole is alive and in action; the scene perpetually changing, but in its changes exhibits an order more striking than could be made to arise from the mere position or description of any form entirely at rest." In reality, "the principles of agitation and of life combine their effects in constituting an order of things, which is at once *fleeting and permanent*."[88] Thus, not only is the "whole *alive* and in *action*," but the movement of this life takes a dialectical shape. "While the things that were are passing away, things that were not are brought into being."[89]

Ferguson modifies this classical understanding of nature by infusing it with Providence. The natural world is God's creation, and like the artist who gives every effort to preserve his masterpiece, so too does God concern himself with the care of his good world. It is indeed a natural world enlivened by the immanent Spirit "consisting" in Christ (Col. 1:17). The life-cycle of nature reflects the *telos* of divine wisdom in its paradoxical character: material and immaterial, describable and indescribable, fleeting and permanent. Life-cycle as a natural revelation of God imitates the revelation of the gospel of Jesus Christ, whose life, death, and resurrection restores the created order and reconciles all life from estrangement. But the transformation of creation that follows from the resurrection of Christ does not emanate a progressive hue; "redemption" conveys a meaning that definitively avoids the ambitions of progress. His world was created good (Genesis 1) and does not need to be improved upon, only ordered.[90]

Semblances of improvement making appearance in history—perceived in the only way improvements or declines can be perceived, retrospectively—are the direct result of Christianity's inexhaustible competence for transforming human existence. Transformations are often interpreted as improvements, and indeed this is not to a fault, since many important historical moments disclose obvious progresses. The trouble, however, is that what may seem an example of progress from one vantage point may well appear an odious corruption from another.[91] Progresses, if they occur at all, occupy only a minor niche of human experience and invariably suffer a very short life. Confusion sets in

---

88. Ferguson, *Principles*, vol. I, 174 (emphasis mine).

89. Ibid., 175.

90. For more on the logic of providence that emerges from the resurrection see Oliver O'Donovan, *Resurrection and Moral Order* (Grand Rapids: Eerdmans, 1986).

91. "The attempt to know what we have not means of knowing is an infallible way to generate illusions; and this attempt to judge whether one period of history or phase of human life, taken as a whole, shows progress as compared with its predecessor, generates illusions of an easily recognizable type" (Collingwood, *Idea of History*, 327)

when a "change" observed in history is categorized positively or negatively according to some unknown evaluative criteria. Prescriptions of what should or should not have been the case will therefore dismember any history it interprets. More important than the historical change itself, however, is the inner meaning of that change partially hidden from scrutiny. *Meaning*, not fact, is the crux of historical knowledge. Whether persons or societies progress to superior states of being is less important historically than seeking to recover the significance of historical phenomena by asking what has actually been accomplished. Meaning emerges from eruptive newness in history. "To be truly 'history,'" as Oliver O'Donovan has put it, "history must be shaped by the unique, by that which cannot be guessed from the scrutiny of the natural."[92] When the artist completes his masterpiece on canvas he revisits it only with the most delicate and meticulous strokes.

Perhaps the most questionable consequence of the conjectural model in the modern age is its packaging of progress into economic theory. The totalizing intensity with which the economy demands our constant attention tends also to blind us to the fact that nearly all capitalist models have in-built variables of progress. The market must expand, consumption increase, and ever more capital generated. Unrelenting in its aspirations, the progressive market is incapable of yielding to its own demands; its thirst is unquenchable. Christian virtues of contentment, satisfaction, peace, and generosity are banished into exile. This is not to say, of course, that capitalism would self-destruct if guided by such virtues; it may well be strengthened. The point, rather, is that under present conditions the progressive energy of capitalism discourages (or disallows) these Christian virtues. Liberal free market capitalism promises limitless horizons for limitless human ambitions, and we have arrived at this position, however indirectly, precisely because progress came to describe what happens necessarily to the world over time.

History is a search for meaning, and meaning endeavors to express itself uniquely in history. For Ferguson, history is not a story of progress—history is a sage. Through its lens one traces the moral and political contours of human existence. History resists rigid determinacy and is absorbed into Providence, which preserves history by infusing it with meaning. Commercial progress may improve certain political institutions or it may ruin them; one can never be certain. Civilizations rise and fall, institutions endure and crumble, societies unite and dissolve. What is to come of any given society cannot be determined absolutely, and for this reason Ferguson recommends a posture of humility.

---

92. O'Donovan, *Resurrection and Moral Order*, 83.

People of one age cannot with any degree of accuracy claim superiority to another when comprehensive evaluative criteria remain unavailable. Bound up in the wisdom of God, history is, in truth, the story of his goodness; a symphony of which he is the author, conductor, and audience: History bespeaks him as he reveals its meaning.

3

Action and Human Nature

Historians familiar with eighteenth-century moral and political thought might balk at the proposal of treating action as an exceptional philosophic category. The eighteenth century, they will say, is the age of natural reason, Greek virtue, and Roman politics; the age of moral sense, sentiment, sympathy, fellow-feeling, and natural reason. If the period erects any ideological pillars, action is not likely to be one of them. For most eighteenth-century philosophers, action is at best a tertiary concern. One acts in the way one is conditioned or determined to act. Studying the act itself can illuminate little of moral or political significance. This tendency toward evaluation of pre-action conditions is perhaps the most dominant motif of eighteenth-century moral philosophy, and it is precisely in light of this motif and philosophers' determination to marginalize the role of action in moral and political theory that Ferguson's thought becomes all the more unique. Unlike his Scottish contemporaries, Ferguson positions action squarely in the center of his philosophical investigations. He is concerned with practical questions his contemporaries either neglect or purposefully marginalize. Action is not merely a by-product of other more important ethical matters, but a moral and political gateway through which all practical investigations must pass.

Unique he may be; systematic he most certainly is not. Ferguson's is a conceptually cautious and historically balanced action theory of subtle originality, charily weaving together disparate threads of classical insight and Christian metaphysical reflection. We saw in the previous chapter that "active being" occupied a prominent, if not a central position in Ferguson's philosophy of history: action is understood historically and history is largely understood as a narrative of actions. To better define the texture of action in Ferguson's project, therefore, this essay will begin by reviewing several of Ferguson's peers—Hutcheson, Hume, and Smith—and outlining briefly their rationale for centralizing virtue in civil society, taking particular note of how action fell into disfavor as a moral subject during the period. Each of these theorists view action as an inessential part of moral philosophy, and in the final estimate it will be crucial to see why this was the case. With these contextual observations in place, a sketch of Ferguson's own action theory will be provided with greater specificity, focusing narrowly on five distinct but interrelated conceptual themes: history, human nature, reason, virtue, and futurity. Framing the sketch within these thematic parameters will aid in further illustrating Ferguson's distinctiveness as a thinker and will accentuate the Christian character of his action theory. At the conclusion of this rehearsal it will be essential to put some conceptual distance between Ferguson and the Roman Stoicism to which he has been linked by modern commentators, and to highlight the significance that his crudely existential understanding of action has for commerce and for the types of exertions called for commercially in political life. If action could be said to have an essence, does that essence reflect certain Christian commitments? If so, how do those commitments produce moral shape in the commercial sphere?

Interlocutors: Scottish Contemporaries and Ancient Stoicism

Eighteenth-century philosophy, on the whole, has comparatively little to say about the nature or anatomy of action and incomparably more to say about the nature of virtue. Not dissimilar to previous ages for which virtue takes conceptual priority, moral inquiry in the eighteenth century tends to bypass transformative action altogether by focusing on what lies hidden behind actions in the form of passions or dispositions. Scottish moralists of this period were of no exception and were perhaps even *more* predisposed to privilege virtue over exertive action in moral casuistry. Before proceeding to a reconstruction and interpretation of Ferguson's theory of action, therefore, it would be useful first to capture a vision of how several Scottish peers—in this case Francis Hutcheson, David Hume, and Adam Smith—conceived of the virtue-action interface.

The philosophic contributions of Francis Hutcheson could be viewed as a preliminary attempt to break apart and differentiate the dispositional strata upholding impassioned virtue. Questions relating to the appropriate execution or intended goals of action are no longer relevant or interesting. His attention is narrowed to the discrete origins of action where passions offer singular guidance to particular moral judgments. The main strategy of his *Inquiry into the Origins of Our Ideas of Beauty and Virtue* demonstrates that virtue is comprehended by human nature's *moral sense*—"that faculty by which we perceive virtue and vice, and approve or disapprove of them in others."[1] This sense of virtue or vice is itself reducible to "one general foundation; the manner [of] computing the morality of Actions."[2] By making Moral Sense the basic origin of action and diverting the focus of moral inquiry to questions of why and how the Moral Sense operates, Hutcheson enshrines a cognitive function that serves as both the executor *and* object of moral evaluation. The pursuit of moral learning becomes a retreat into the mind's Moral Sense, and the task of moral deliberation becomes an exercise in describing dispositional attitudes. Contingent mental content temporarily controlling the Moral Sense is of greatest ethical significance. The "intention of Moral Philosophy," he claims, is "to direct men to that course of action which tends most effectually to promote their greatest happiness and perfection; as far as it can be done by observations and conclusions discoverable from the constitution of nature, without any aids of supernatural revelation."[3] Moral inquiry therefore addresses the fluctuating properties of an otherwise constant Moral Sense.

Nevertheless, the true and happy end of humankind "cannot be distinctly known without previous knowledge of the constitution of the species," which we are told later is simply "to inquire into the several powers and dispositions of the species."[4] Strangely, this investigation into (historically) "previous" dispositions is never conducted. Hutcheson instead attempts to translate historically sensitive moral concepts into terms suitable for the ever-widening field of contemporary "pneumatics."[5] The important task, he thinks, is to describe the mental faculty of moral sense and why that faculty approves or disapproves of certain actions. Such approbation, in the end, is all that matters in morality: "There is therefore . . . a *natural* and *immediate* determination to approve certain affections, and actions consequent upon them; or a natural sense of immediate excellence in them, *not referred to any other quality perceivable by our other senses or by reasoning*."[6] With the appearance of "approval" language, one recognizes the functions of a learned and immediate "determination" (judgment) operating unfettered from reasoning, law, truth, or history.[7] This cluster of instincts (senses) and judgments known as human nature are

---

1. Francis Hutcheson, *An Inquiry into the Original of Our Ideas of Beauty and Virtue* (Indianapolis: Liberty Fund, 2004), treatise II, section 1.

2. Ibid., treatise II, section 3.

3. Francis Hutcheson, *A System of Moral Philosophy* (London: Continuum, 2006).

4. Ibid., book I, chapter 1.

5. It is perhaps no small irony that "Pneumatics," or study of the Spirit of Mind, is in eighteenth-century Scottish literature wholly unaccepting of "supernatural aids."

6. Ibid., book I, chapter 3 (emphasis mine).

considered absolutely trustworthy and universally benevolent, cooperating "beautifully" to maximize personal and corporate happiness.[8] It is simply a credit to the Author of nature that benevolence happens to be that affection which most directly leads to human happiness.

David Hume, on the other hand, though certainly partial to a "pneumatic" method, attempts to get behind even the moral sense itself by explaining what it is and to what it is not ultimately beholden. Moral philosophy interrogates the collection of perceptions causally linked to feelings of pleasure and pain. Like Hutcheson, Hume also detaches the virtuousness of an action from its reasonableness. On his account, the problem is "whether it be possible, from reason alone, to distinguish betwixt moral good and evil, or whether there must concur some other principles to enable us to make that distinction."[9] Morals are transformed from objective authorities to special intellectual powers, since reason lacks the causal capacity to initiate an action from its own resources and must instead rely upon the forces of passion and perception to accomplish its ends. Hume's more extreme claim that "moral distinctions are not the offspring of reason," which understands reason to be "wholly inactive," further reinforces the virtue-action contrast.[10] These stark divisions between reason and morality, and between virtue and action, signal the final and "natural" conclusion that "morality is more properly *felt* than judged of."[11] Feeling and the perception of feeling actually *constitute* praise or blame.[12] By making human nature the decisive authority of moral inquiry, Hume has reduced the totality of ethical content to natural human passions by collapsing the role of deliberative reason. On his view, not only must reason remain mute within moral discourses, but so

7. In the text leading up to the quotation provided from book 1, chapter 3 of *A System of Moral Philosophy*, Hutcheson lists several features of classical moral philosophy with which his brand of pneumatical morality has little to do, law and truth included!

8. Hutcheson's anticipation of Utilitarianism is nowhere more strongly expressed than in his *Inquiry* (II, 3): "In comparing the moral quality of actions in order to regulate our elections among various actions proposed, or to find which of them has the greatest moral excellence, we are led by our moral sense of virtue to judge thus: that in equal degrees of happiness, expected to proceed from the action, the virtue is in proportion to the number of persons to whom the happiness shall extend . . . so that that action is best which procures the greatest happiness for the greatest numbers . . ."

9. David Hume, *A Treatise on Human Nature*, ed. L. A. Selby-Bigge (Oxford: Clarendon, 1978) book III, part i, section 1.

10. Ibid.

11. Book III, part i, section 2.

12. Ibid. Hume's argument for the "feeling" of virtue is nowhere better expressed than in section 2 of part i (book III): "We do not infer a character to be virtuous because it pleases: but in feeling that it pleases after such a particular manner, we in effect feel that it is virtuous."

too must virtue, as it is absorbed into the feelings of personal association. Virtue is nothing but the feeling of pleasure, and vice nothing but the feeling of pain.[13] The meaning of virtue in turn signifies empirical principles of mind habituated and organized into a personal "character." "Actions themselves," Hume insists, "not proceeding from any constant principle have no influence on love or hatred, pride or humility; and consequently are never considered in morality."[14] Hence, all genuine ethical inquiry is concerned with the quality of character from which action proceeded; no other origin is possible.

Passions eventually give rise to sympathy and to a specific kind of pleasure that only the sympathetic can enjoy. Sympathy is for Hume the highest and most basic moral faculty. Functioning much like the moral sense, sympathy is socially informed and causally constructed, approving or disapproving as passions dictate. Human beings within civil society learn to accommodate one another by expressing and enjoying mutual sympathy. This is why he is able to redefine justice as an interior (artificial) virtue and law as a perpetuation of social custom; both justice and law become expressions of how impassioned individuals secure social cohesion through formal institutions. By universalizing human nature in this way he can parse his treatment of virtue and vice (methodologically) into two distinct parts; the *nature* of virtue and vice on the one hand, and the *function* of virtue and vice on the other.[15] Human nature is fashioned into a function that both receives and contributes "extensive sympathy" and "limited generosity," because "moral good and evil are certainly distinguished by our *sentiments*, and not our *reason*."[16] Thus, if a passion contributes to an enduring beauty, then that passion is found immediately agreeable and absolutely trustworthy.

One of Hume's many aims is to eradicate action from moral inquiry altogether by identifying what he believes holds the true power of being—human nature. Two implications of Hume's theory of human nature merit further consideration: the internalization of value and the social ascription of identity. The internalization of value is most clearly expounded in his *Essays*. In a sequence of four essays, Hume enlists the ancient philosophic schools—Epicurean, Stoic, Platonist, and Skeptic—to face down rationalist phantoms in seventeenth- and eighteenth-century moral epistemology. Of those antiquarian schools represented, Hume unreservedly casts his lot with

13. Ibid.

14. Book III, part iii, section 1.

15. The three parts into which book III of Hume's *Treatise* is divided: "Of Virtue and Vice in General," "Of Justice and Injustice," and "Of the Other Virtues and Vices."

16. Book III, part i, section 2.

the Skeptics. The Epicurean, or "the man of elegance and pleasure," makes pleasure the object of pursuit and pain the object of his avoidance; the Stoic, or "the man of action and virtue," attempts to abolish desire altogether, or at the least become indifferent to it; the Platonist, or "the man of contemplation and philosophical devotion," hopes for mind to find happiness in its most perfect object; the Skeptic, on the other hand, harbors doubt about the whole externality of an ultimate or universal object. As Hume puts it, "In a word, human life is more governed by fortune than by reason; is to be regarded more as a dull pastime than as a serious occupation; and is more influenced by particular humor, than by general principles."[17] No first principles exist that are not already qualities of mind, for "it is not from the value or worth of the object which any person pursues, that we can determine his enjoyment, but merely from the passion with which he pursues it, and the success which he meets with in his pursuit."[18] One must get on with one's life as best one can. Look inside! Out there, "objects have absolutely no worth or value in themselves."[19]

Adam Smith's moral theory, as the title of his monograph on moral philosophy suggests, also overlooks the performance of action. Virtue consists in the complementarity, or coherence, of virtues within the Impartial Spectator. The meaning of an action is immediately comprehended by the Impartial Spectator as virtuous or vicious, praiseworthy or blameworthy, and only she can determine whether an action has upheld the "rules" of perfect prudence, strict justice, and proper benevolence.[20] From what do these "rules" of perfect prudence arise? To what are they essentially associated? On his account, the rules are ontologically bound up with the intellectual faculty that evaluates moral character, the principle of approbation. Never clearly defined, the principle of approbation refers to that faculty approving or disapproving of experienced phenomena according to understood rules of virtue. Like Hume, Smith's notion of approbation includes an element of judgment; unlike Hume, it does not rest upon grounds of utility or beauty, but upon prudence, the very unity of "superior reason" and self-command.[21]

17. See essays XV–XVIII in David Hume's *Essays Moral, Political and Literary*, ed. E. F. Miller (Indianapolis: Liberty Fund, 1987).

18. Ibid., 166.

19. Ibid.

20. Identifying what determines an action's success in upholding the "perfect, strict, and proper" rules would go a long way toward making sense of Smith's conceptual division. Is it the rules, or the judgment of the rules, that determines virtue? See Adam Smith, *The Theory of Moral Sentiments*, ed. D. D. Raphael and A. L. Macfie (Indianapolis: Liberty Fund, 1982).

21. Smith's explicit criticism of Hume's utility principle is conducted in part IV, ch. 2 of *Theory of Moral Sentiments*.

> When we approve of any character or action, the sentiments which
> we feel are . . . derived from four sources: [i] we sympathize with the
> motives of the agent; [ii] we enter into the gratitude of those who
> receive the benefit of action; [iii] we observe that his conduct has
> been agreeable to the general rules by which those two sympathies
> generally act; and [iv] we consider such actions as making a part of
> a system of behavior which tends to promote the happiness either of
> the individual or of the society . . .[22]

How this inductive process of entirely natural sentimental negotiation finds its
true heartbeat in repeated evaluative judgments remains ill-defined. Judgment is
not identical to action. For Smith, action is an opportunity to demonstrate that
one has rightly empathized with, and thus adapted to, the demands of society.
Of supreme importance, as it was for Hutcheson and Hume, are the origins
of action grounded in a principle of sentimental approbation. Action itself is
politically and legally, but not *morally*, interesting or applicable.

FERGUSON ON THE MEANING OF ACTION

We are now in a position to consider Ferguson's theory of action in its Scottish
and Stoic context. As a way of re-presenting his action theory as *respondent
to* and not wholly dependent upon these conceptual inheritances, the
interpretation I wish to proffer identifies five conceptual signposts anchoring
and orienting active being: (i) history, (ii) human nature, (iii) reason, (iv) virtue,
and (v) futurity. Framing the theory in this way will carry the constructive
advantage of revealing the *transcendent* nature of action that provokes obedient
endeavors into Godliness.

That the concept of action is integral to Ferguson's philosophical project is
beyond any reasonable contention. The priority of action is asserted repeatedly:

> To act in the view of his fellow-creatures, to produce his mind in
> public, to give it all the exercise of sentiment and thought, which
> pertain to man as a member of society, as a friend, or an enemy,
> seems to be the principal calling and occupation of his nature. If he
> must labour, that he may subsist, he can subsist for no better purpose

22. Ibid., part VII, ch. 3, pt. iii.

than the good of mankind; nor can he have better talents than those which qualify him to act with men.[23]

Or, similarly:

> Men are to be estimated not from what they know, but from what they are able to perform; from their skill in adapting materials to the several purposes of life; from their vigour and conduct in pursuing the objects of policy, and in finding the expedients of war and national defence.[24]

Indeed, "the happiness of men, in all cases alike, consists in the blessings of a candid, an active, and strenuous mind."[25] Active being plays a dominant role in Ferguson's moral thought precisely because action is dominant to life itself. He is a practical man interested in practical subjects. Of what good is philosophical inquiry if it cannot tell us how best to live our lives? He has little patience for disproportionate speculation or playful theorizing, seeing as "[t]he parade of words, and general reasonings, which sometimes carry an appearance of so much learning and knowledge, are of little avail in the conduct of life."[26] Yet when the imperative *that* one must act is readily accepted and deliberations brought to a close, where does that leave us? Is anything else of conceptual or practical consequence to the execution of acts?

Of particular interest here is the history of the agent and the reality into which she acts. Every active moment is directly rooted in temporally prior moments supported always by a collective memory applicable to the task at hand. Most personal skills are in fact cultivated and preserved in this manner; learning to walk, drive, read, and speak are first observed and soon followed by attempts of our own. Memory and habits are cooperative partners in tasks of propriety, and yet neither is identical to nor independent of the other. Habits require a kind of memory that is not rightly called memory but rather a *surpassing* of memory—the casting of memory in a semi-permanent mold. Memory is essential to action; habit inessential. The latter makes action easier; the former makes it possible. Habit is the ingrained memory of how to act without direct attention, while memory is the force giving action its energy and

23. Adam Ferguson, *Essay on the History of Civil Society*, ed. Fania Oz-Salzberger (Cambridge: Cambridge University Press, 2007), 33.

24. Ibid.

25. Ibid., 60.

26. Ibid., 31.

course. Memory and habit contextualize actions by putting each act in touch with a history that speaks to the present.

History discloses to the historian facts that collectively comprise the story of being. Past events express themselves as "facts" in that if an event has occurred, then the properties and effects of that event communicate what has transpired as a matter of actual historical occurrence. In this sense anything in the past can be history to the extent that it discloses intelligible content to the present. History cannot perpetuate itself apart from the *memory* of an affected people. Yet memory always runs the risk of being forgotten, altered, or helplessly misrepresented; although the facts that support it can never be abolished volitionally.[27] If ever an event was at any time apprehended by the human mind, there is a chance that it will forever endure and stand as a mighty oak in the firmament of the past. If forgotten, however, the oak returns to the dust from which it came and the living past along with it. Memories of the past challenge their indeterminacy by continually breaking through to the present. Truths of past events, despite being upheld beyond time by the Divine mind, are in the created order contingent upon indeterminacies of the human mind—rooted in the shifting sand of its often unreliable memory holders.

And yet it is within this tension of factual past and uncertain memory that the task of historiography recommends itself. History, for Ferguson, is a story of *active* being. Past actions and events recommend diverse possibilities and the latent obligations couched within them. The stories of action arise from history as an authoritative tutor to the present moral and political spheres.[28] "The order of things consists in *movements*," claims Ferguson, "which in a state of counteraction and apparent disturbance, mutually regulate and balance one another."[29] Historically conceived, this "order" is the direct result of a dialectical relationship between *exertion* and *opposition*, and thus the "movement" of history tells a story of humans encountering and overcoming opposition in

---

27. For what is easily among the greatest of treatments ever given to the nature of memory, see book X of St. Augustine's *Confessions*, trans. F. J. Sheed (Indianapolis: Hackett, 2007).

28. One may think here of Barth's masterful reflection on history in *Protestant Theology in the Nineteenth Century* (London: SCM, 1972): "We know history only when and in that something happens in us and for us, perhaps even happens against us; we know it only when and in that event concerns us, so concerns us that we are there, that we participate in it. Any knowledge of history that proved to be merely seeing, observing, establishing, is a contradiction in itself. Certainly the knowledge of human action—*and that is what history is about*—involves seeing, observing, establishing, but not in isolated theory. . . . We know history in that another's action somehow becomes a question to which our own action has to give some sort of answer" (emphasis mine, 15–16).

29. Adam Ferguson, *Principles of Moral and Political Science* (New York: Garland, 1978), vol. 1, 18 (emphasis mine).

a way that transforms a given state of affairs. The movement of history—the passage of time—is composed of a symphony of active beings playing different parts in different places at different times and with varying measures of concerted harmony. Whether one holds the cello bow or the conductor's baton, making an impression on the narrative history of active being is simply a matter of taking up one's instrument and putting it into motion.

The past carried memorably into present actions is what Ferguson identifies as the "history of active being."[30] To say something sensible about humankind's present condition it is incumbent to say something about what man has been like: actions simply cannot be identified as good or evil, virtuous or vicious, agreeable or disagreeable without a historical backdrop against which to contrast or contextualize them. Apart from a historical background the portrait of action remains unintelligible. Hutcheson, Hume, and Smith all believed that the way to conduct a natural history of action is to peel back layers of the intending mind.[31] Ferguson's archaeology of action, on the other hand, differs methodologically from his contemporaries' in that it does not appeal to cognitive functions for answers to the questions of the history of active being, resisting the search for mind's causal ghosts. Without first conducting a *genuinely* historical exploration of active being—an exploration of what human actions have expressed over time, that is—commonality is lost and the meaning of action eroded. The history of active being discloses the exertions of a plurality of men among and for a plurality of men. Obvious as it may seem, the distinction here is subtle. If, as was the view of his contemporaries, the method for uncovering a history of active being is to classify psychological causes or principles of pre-action processes, then the only meaningful results of philosophical interest will be the collection of memories and quality of intellectual faculties afforded to *that particular person*. Thus, claiming that the history of active being is in truth a history of human nature is to begin with what is already a categorical mistake. Understanding how man has acted must be gleaned by an appeal to man's active history *in reality*, not to hypothetical states of mind prior to action.

30. As noted above, the *Essay*, *Institutes*, and *Principles* all begin with treatments of man's active history.

31. Admittedly, Hume had his own reservations about the prospects of this strategy, though he believed the problem to be surmountable in the end: "It is remarkable concerning the operations of the mind that though most intimately present to us, yet, whenever they become the object of reflexion, they seem involved in obscurity; nor can the eye readily find those lines and boundaries which discriminate and distinguish them." See *Enquiry Concerning Human Understanding* (Oxford: Clarendon, 1988), 13. Later, of course, Hume explains that this "uncertain and chimerical" science must still be undertaken as far as is possible.

Action is a deeply social phenomenon. Discovery of human nature is not achieved through isolated self-reflection, desperately peeling back ontological layers in search of mind's elusive intellectual phantoms. One best comes to terms with the significance of action by presenting oneself to others in society and then seeking to understand the action's wider meaning in historical and political terms. Ferguson's *Essay* illustrates this point rather clearly. Understanding the present is achieved by appealing to past actions chronicled in public memory. Any meaningful history is nothing *less* than the history of active being, just as any meaningful action is nothing less than action historically disclosed. Likewise, history is defined by the shape and force of actions past, just as actions are defined by the history brought to bear upon them through memory; it is how the two understand one another. The content of history is written by action, and the content of action is written by history.

With this historically enriched theory of active being in mind, to what extent is human nature strictly natural? Ferguson is disparaging of a purely "pneumatic" theory of human nature and prefers instead a historical model that locates the regularities and continuities of action across time. For a particular action to be considered "natural" to mankind it must be fundamentally habitual or customary. One might be tempted to call these habitual or cultural inclinations "instincts." This would be a mistaken redefinition, however, and would identify "the natural" with purely subjective powers and overlook the instructive forces of reality and civil society. Action is learned from society, and once learned it is *for* society that action is recommitted. Over time this giving and receiving is engrained and hardened, becoming man's natural setting within society. "To be in society is the physical state of the species. . . . It is the state of those who quarrel, as well as those who agree. Estrangement is not always a vice, nor association a virtue."[32]

Early in the *Principles* Ferguson challenges the problem of ahistorical pneumatics—when pneumatics precedes historiography—by questioning introspective appeals to "pure" human nature. Attempts by his contemporaries to get behind the virtues actually turn out to be historical descriptions of an agent's sentiments "entertained in view of his species."[33] Both Hume and Smith admittedly place great emphasis on the basic sociality of individual agency, though it is not the basic sociality of man Ferguson is here calling into question. Human nature *alone* cannot define the order of community, but neither is community the sole determinant of human nature. Identifying "sympathy" or

---

32. *Principles*, 24.

33. Ibid., 10 (i.e., natural history).

"sentiment" as the seat of human nature simply begs the question. Upon what is sentiment founded? What are its justifying conditions? The sentimentalization of human action mistakenly exalts human nature (pneumatically conceived) as an entity unto itself, a throne from which the soul renders conclusive moral judgments. Human nature, insists Ferguson, cannot be reduced to basic motivational passions. Passions may, and often do contribute to the process of deliberate action, but if they are made to *constitute* the moral goodness or badness of an action, then it is upon these passions that the blame or praise is finally laid. The problem with this position is that an agent's intention is entirely unobservable even to the most "impartial" spectator. Motivation is not displayed externally for public judgment. Modern law enforcement observes this truth when prosecuting perpetrators whose motive may help explain proximately, but never conclusively, the offender's ultimate guilt or innocence. Explicating motivations cannot satisfy the question of "why?" The concealment of intentionality from the public means it is always possible that what may first appear a benevolent action is in fact reprehensibly selfish, or what may appear cruel to have the saintliest of motives. Only God and the acting agent can be certain.

Against this type of argument, basing the goodness or badness of an act upon the passion from which it proceeded, Ferguson advances his principle of unintended consequences: "Mankind, in following the present sense of their minds, in striving to remove inconveniencies, or to gain apparent contiguous advantages, arrive at ends which even their imagination could not anticipate; and pass on, like other animals, in the track of their nature, without perceiving its end."[34] This principle is typically applied to social and political forms in which a society intends one specific objective but inevitably actualizes several other states of affairs by accident. Indeterminacy of this sort alerts us to a stark and largely unbridgeable distance separating action from intention at both a political and personal level. At the political level, for example, when elevating conquest, riches, and glory to principal aims for ever-widening territorial expansion, ancient Rome certainly did not *intend* to compromise its capital city tactically by inadvertently spreading its military forces too thin. Compromising its beloved heartland was in this case an unintended consequence of inexorable ambition and domestic inattention. Likewise, on a personal level, a decision to go trekking in the Highlands for the purpose of refreshment and adventure might at the same time cause one's spouse to feel a sense of abandonment and insensitivity to marital responsibility.[35] One not infrequently finds that

---

34. Ibid., 118.

enthusiasm, to cite yet another example, can easily (and often) be taken by others as severe aggression or perverse arrogance, and not at all like genuine excitement.

The distinction to be drawn here is not that actions and intentions are incommensurable, but that intentions cannot control the *effects* of action. Action serves rather like a buffer between intention and effect that can fully adapt to arbitrate communications. An action's moral worth cannot reside in the sum-total of that action's motivational content.

Ferguson's theory of action also embodies certain metaphysical commitments. Freedom, on his account, is best described conceptually as "dialectical": true freedom finds its fullest expression in rightful limitations, just as rightful limitations find fullest expression in freedom. Limitation gives meaning to freedom, and freedom gives meaning to limitation. Confinement and freedom are to man "the principal constituents of good or of evil," for without freedom and confinement the labeling of actions as good or evil would be meaningless.[36] Consider three fixtures of this dialectical relationship between freedom and limitation, the last of which will return us to our main discussion: law, divine foreknowledge, and reason.

Reality governs humanity with physical laws and political laws. Physical laws determine what is and is not physically possible; that is, my throwing a baseball from here to the moon, willing myself to atomically disintegrate, and so forth. Political laws, by and large, protect and preserve the public good and limit the types of action contributing to societal degradation. Together these different types of law provide a context for meaningful action. Laws determine what is or is not, should or should not be in one's freedom to decide. We might call these limitations that we have no say over "determinations from above." "Determinations from below," on the other hand, are limits placed on an agent by his own physical and intellectual capacity. Only so many actions are available to a person at any one time. My becoming perfectly virtuous by this afternoon's coffee, for example, is as impossible as my solving calculus equations in theoretical astrophysics. These possibilities are not (realistically)

---

35. One may think here of St. Paul's exhortation to the church at Rome where he confesses that—"I cannot understand my own behavior . . . I fail to carry out the things I want to do, and I find myself doing the very things I hate" (Rom. 7:15, NJB). It is worth noting that, for Paul, action must be held in relation to Law, as he explains in the very next verse (v. 16): "When I act against my own will, that means I have a self that acknowledges that the Law is good, and so the thing behaving in that way is not my self but sin living in me." Paul's instruction applies to the relationship between action and intention, not action and effect; doing what ought not be done and, in turn, not doing what ought to be done.

36. Ibid., 124.

available to me because neither is in my *capacity* to achieve, not because reality itself places limitations. Yet despite being limited from "above" and "below," agency often means exercising specific freedoms over both reality (above) and the self (below).[37] To exercise freedom in this way, however, requires reason, which leads us to the third concept to which action is oriented in Ferguson's theory.

Reason is inseparable from our previous two action-oriented concepts of history and human nature. For Hume, the reader will recall, reason is "wholly inactive" in morality and should not enter into our contemplation of good or evil. Hutcheson and Smith, though not as explicit in their separation of passion from reason, create a similar division, which claims that virtue consists in particular "sentiments." Such "sentimentalization" of morality partly explains the mature moral psychology supporting these texts, especially Hume's *Treatise* and *Enquiries* and Smith's *Theory of Moral Sentiments*. When reason is thought slave to the passions it becomes clear why moralists would be dissuaded to include reason as a central function in ethical theory, especially when reason appears in nature to be ethically neutral. But is it really the case that morality is "better felt than judged of"? Ferguson responds to this question in the negative, and for three reasons: the separation of reason from morality confuses our understanding of (i) freedom, (ii) casuistry, and (iii) judgment.

What is freedom without reason? To be faced with an authentic decision is to have no less than two options from which to decide, a criterion of truth and falsity upholding the agent's relation to reality, and possession of the intellectual faculties needed to see a decision through from inception to completion. Freedom is not the mere absence of restraint, as many modern commentators have liked to insist, but the description given to what is or is not in one's power to act upon in reality.[38] Both the circumstances of reality and

37. "He [man] is in some measure the artificer of his own frame, as well as his fortune, and is destined from the first age of his being to invent and contrive. He applies the same talents to a variety of purposes and acts nearly the same part in very different scenes" (*Essay*, 12). And yet, ". . . his particular pursuits are prescribed to him by circumstances of the age and of the country in which he lives: in one situation he is occupied with wars and political deliberations; in another, with the care of his interest, of his personal ease, or conveniency" (161).

38. Oliver O'Donovan has argued that moral freedom "can never be established on the basis of self-sufficiency and independence of the world. Freedom, if it is freedom to act *within* the world, must itself be *of* the world. . . . Reason has its importance only as the agent's means of purchase upon reality, and not in itself: the authority attributed to reason is more properly understood to belong to reality. We speak of 'authority.' The real world authorizes man's agency in general by being the context of its exercise, and his particular acts by being the context in which they have a point." *Resurrection and the Moral Order* (Grand Rapids: Eerdmans, 1986), 120.

capacity of the agent give shape to action's possibilities, as Ferguson observes: "in any two situations [the agent] must ever vary his pursuits, and accommodate his manner of life to the exigency of his case."[39] Complex moral situations confront us with dilemmas and quandaries that no amount of impassioned virtue can assist in making the truthful moral decision about. Volition may very well contribute a dominant power to our exertions, but it should never be *identified* with pure passion. Reason always, to a lesser or greater degree, accompanies the emergence of a willful act.[40] To be free is to have it within one's power to decide and act upon a given state of affairs, and "by this law of his nature, he is entrusted to himself as the clay is entrusted to the hands of the potter."[41] Freedom is thus a law of human nature one is forever compelled to obey. Truth and falsity authoritatively structure practical reason, and practical reason in turn structures freedom. To act freely is to have it within one's power to act rightly or wrongly; that is, to have one's action sanctioned by the same criterion of truth that authorized and legitimated the initial decision. There are unique goods found in reasonable living, and each must "observe and . . . choose among the objects around him; to make a trial of different practices; and to abide by that which is most suited to his circumstances, or to the situation in which he is *placed*."[42] In short, rational deliberation is a condition to the possibility of authentic freedom, since to act without thought is already to have acted irresponsibly.

Practical deliberation about the kinds of actions one can and should rationally undertake leads to considerations of *how* laws structuring human affairs are rightly understood. Reason's casuistic office has to do with the perception, interpretation, and application of external laws of morality. Casuistry brings subject and reality together at a moral crossroads—seeing the way things are in the world and *thinking* about how best to engage them. But what, exactly, is to be interpreted? What is the rightful goal of casuistry? If, as Ferguson suggests, "[a]ll nature is connected, and the world itself consists of parts, which, like the stones of an arch, mutually support and are supported," then shouldn't the moral hermeneutic one employs hold *order* as its object? To know how to do what is right in any given situation requires provisional

39. *Principles*, 57.

40. Ultimately, as will be seen later, the freedom of agency must be infused with the freedom found in God.

41. Ibid., 225.

42. Ibid., 232 (emphasis mine). As will be seen later, the confrontation of agent with reality is never arbitrary or superfluous and is never wholly up to personal choice, but is an encounter "given" by "placement."

knowledge of the conditions that must be satisfied in order to perform the action rightly. Observation, interpretation, and execution all depend on right reason and sound judgment. As Ferguson eloquently puts it, the aim is "to penetrate the order established in nature; to emulate this order . . . to unfold the principles of estimation, and realize the conceptions of excellence and beauty, in works to be executed by human art. . . ."[43] Morality can no more rid itself of reason than the farmer can his plow. Reason is the instrument that unearths what is good and truthful about human action, and it is incumbent on each to recognize that "human reason cannot finally acquiesce in what is found to be evil."[44] Nor, for that matter, should one refrain from doing what one knows to be good.

Deliberation of moral concepts must eventually narrow at the gateway of judgment. Judgment is considered a "gateway" in that it is primarily through judgment that reasoning passes into action. Actions pass through the gateway of judgment and with passage thus become decidedly moral, immoral, or amoral. Judgment, as it were, makes action rational and the rational performable. For Ferguson, "moral judgments give *sanction* to the propriety of . . . character or action in the society of fellow creatures"; that is, within the context of society, moral judgments assign moral worth to character and actions.[45] The meaning of "propriety" in the eighteenth century did not signify what has in contemporary parlance come to mean "acceptable"; rather, the eighteenth century held strongly to the older, classical definition of propriety as "appropriateness," or "fittedness." In part I, chapter 2, section ix of the *Institutes*, Ferguson defines practical judgment in terms resonant with "foresight":

> Foresight is the faculty of conjecturing what is to follow from the past and present. It requires penetration and sagacity: the first, to comprehend all the circumstances of the case in question; the second, to perceive what is likely to follow from those circumstances. Penetration and sagacity are the foundations of good conduct, art, and skill.[46]

What I would like to suggest is that foresight, as Ferguson defines it, is inseparably bound to deliberative judgment. The same terms used here,

43. Ibid., 206.
44. Ibid., 298.
45. Ibid., 35.
46. Adam Ferguson, *Institutes of Moral Philosophy* (New York: Garland, 1978), 65.

"penetration," "sagacity," and "art," are all used later in the *Principles* to refer to deliberate judgment.[47] Within the language it is couched, deliberate judgment is implicitly rational. Judgment brings completion to deliberative reasoning and begins the work of executive reasoning: from reasoning about what should be done, to what is now being done.[48] More shall be said about the Stoic inflections of this theory later.

So much then for the first three of our concepts—history, human nature, and reason—and our brief interlude. The fourth concept toward which action is oriented in Ferguson's theory is virtue. For his Scottish contemporaries, passions prompt the will to begin acting, implying that the rightness of an act is determined by the character of an original, causal passion. As Smith put it, this cause is the "man of the breast," the personification of feeling. Actions, on his view, are the causal consequence of impassioned sentiments socially conditioned. Virtuous actions proceed from virtuous sentiments and the latter determines the moral worth of the former.

For Ferguson, however, the passion or condition from which action arises has less to do with moral worth than the excellence or propriety of the action itself. Passions, whether felicitous, miserable, or insipid, are a direct consequence of different types of action. The happiness of man is proportioned "to the exertion and application of his faculties . . . not to his exemption from difficulty or danger, but to the magnanimity, courage, and fortitude with which he *acts*."[49] Indeed, "it is mostly in some *active* exertions that happiness consists."[50] Happiness is the experience accompanying action itself, not a residual by-product. The priority of action to virtue is such that the "proper state of nature . . . is not a condition . . . prior to the exercise of faculties, but procured by their just application."[51]

Subjective turns to "natural" inclination are plagued with ambiguity and only explain why the application of "natural" descriptors to human being "can serve to distinguish nothing," since "all the actions of men are equally a result

47. The reason for the disappearance of the section on "foresight" in the *Principles* is the topic's absorption into other subjects, and in any event, this particular contention only bears indirectly upon my main argument, which is that judgment cooperates with reason in a way that disallows omission from moral inquiry.

48. Expressing judgment as a type of act has been recently reiterated by Oliver O'Donovan in *The Ways of Judgment* (Grand Rapids: Eerdmans, 2005). "Judgment is an act of moral discrimination that pronounces upon a preceding act or existing state of affairs to establish a new public context."

49. *Principles*, 185 (emphasis mine).

50. Ibid., 250.

51. *Essay*, 15.

of his nature."[52] The danger in making passions of human nature the starting point for moral inquiry is that *all* actions are a result of human nature and thus can always be qualified as natural. If an action is natural, then it is thought to be right *simply because* it is natural to perform. Identifying naturalness with rightness therefore incurs the risk of reducing moral inquiry to the cataloguing of passions through personal habituation. Hume, for example, catching sight of this conceptual identification, enlists habit as a tool for assigning virtues to human nature; habits quite literally *make* a person good to the extent that they constrain or enhance passions lying behind them.[53] Ferguson, on the other hand, though sympathetic to the power habits wield, insists that habit "is *not* that by which we are first inclined to act, but a disposition which results from our having *already acted*."[54] "Habit is known to be that, by which the good or bad actions of men remain with them, and become part of their characters."[55] Thus habits are the residue left on active being once the effects of action have made their impression.

Successful cultivation of habits likewise requires certain resistances that can take both an external and internal form; external in the form of adversity or trial in reality, and internal in the form of misdirected desire or intellectual apathy. Ferguson celebrates each encounter with resistance because each occurrence generates an occasion for overcoming challenges. Resistance to actions arises either from the ineptitudes of mind or from the adverse circumstances with which one is faced. Each conflicting occasion can and often does inhibit happiness, and might even explain why happiness cannot be an ultimate object of human nature but only a consequence of action itself. The history of active being is the long story of mankind's perseverance in the face of potential negations, a story whose tragic or comedic climax depends upon whether the new state of being occasioned success or failure. Here again Ferguson's method is dialectical. In forward movements the subject encounters barriers to continuity, resistances, that result in either degradation or improvement. Actions meet resistance to the result of either negation or affirmation, and yet even if one's efforts are negated and all attempts to overcome a particular trial are thwarted, it remains within one's power to rectify what *can* be rectified from the encounter.[56] The coward, of course, will retreat from the ferocity of the trial itself or from the embarrassment that comes from having failed; whereas

---

52. Ibid.

53. How far have we now strayed from Aquinas's view of *law* as that which makes man good! See Article II of Question 90 in *Treatise on Law* (Washington, DC: Regnery, 1956).

54. Ferguson, *Principles*, 209.

55. Ibid., 208.

the courageous will make the active decision to face down adversity with the resilience necessary to act again another day.

For Ferguson, virtues are *active*. Passivity is the road to ruination paved with bricks of luxury.[57] One is challenged with a twofold, or dialectical, capacity of action: Action discloses the character of the actor while simultaneously forming the actor's character. The act is a type of *communication* both to the actor and to the actor's world, because "if virtue be the supreme good, its best and most signal effect is, to communicate and diffuse itself."[58] Thus the meaning or moral significance of virtue for mankind is wholly absorbed into the meaning of action itself, since, as Ferguson has told us, it is in the character of the "supreme good" to "communicate" and "diffuse" itself. The meaning of an action contains far more than can be directly determined by an agent's intentions, means, or ends. No doubt each of these leaves its own mark on the meaning of action, but even when taken collectively these three factors are not enough to determine what an action means. This is because the interpretation of an action can never fall entirely within the jurisdiction of the actor. The "unintended consequences" of an action implies that "[m]any actions of men, by a natural connection with their motives, *discover* a meaning, as an effect discovers its cause."[59]

The capacity of action to carry unintended consequences brings our inquiry to the fifth concept around which action is oriented in Ferguson's theory—futurity. Notorious for its rigid determinism, Stoic materiality suspends the temporal significance of active being, the future is inevitable and its inevitability must be accepted with personal indifference. Such determinacy similarly implicates Hume's strictly causal account of human nature. Both Stoic and Humean visions of the future attach static fixity to action's vexing uncertainty. Actions mean what they were intended to mean and nothing else. However, Ferguson has already made it abundantly clear that freedom is a fact about which man is readily conscious, and "[a]ttempts to support it by argument are nugatory, and attempts to overthrow it by argument are absurd."[60] He will have nothing to do with any metaphysic rendering an action meaningless or attempting to reduce the meaning of action to pure

---

56. ". . . it is a distinction of living natures to carry a principle of active exertion in themselves. They are subject to pressure from external causes, and are acted upon; but they also act, and urge to an end, whether to gain an advantage or remove an inconvenience" (*Principles*, 12).

57. Ferguson's critique of luxury will be outlined in chapter 4.

58. *Essay*, 42.

59. *Principles*, 38 (emphasis mine).

60. Ibid., 152.

intentionality. Even so, every action requires at least a degree of fixity or immutability as an ordered context for the appropriation of meaning. Permanence is essential to understanding the impression an action makes on the fabric of reality. And so action must appear within a context of stable permanence accommodating to its blunt force and inherent creativity to be recognizable. The context of action is not "permanent" *per se*, but enduring; comprised of real fixtures that make action possible.

Reality and action belong communicatively to one another as sentences belong to paragraphs. When a friend tells us he has been fishing all weekend, for example, our minds immediately covet more imaginative furniture. Where did the fishing trip take him? What kind of fishing did he do? How many fish did he catch? Our mind casts its nets to gather as much imagery as will help form an idea of what the action means. By virtue of having a place, action can be interpreted for its uniformity or uniqueness, merit or demerit, praiseworthiness or blameworthiness. As another example, it seems a fact of human existence that "the sentence of nature is equally pronounced upon all, that the longest liver must die," and yet the dust to which one returns is, as the Stoics took pains to point out, always entirely within the hands of the agent.[61] The necessity of death and the fact that death is always one's own-most possession illustrate vividly the complex relation between freedom and contexts for action. Other less extreme examples might also be proposed: the writing of a poem, passing judgment on a case, or even driving an automobile. All such actions, though done freely, must observe and respect the laws guiding their performance. Poems follow certain meters, judgments adhere to civil procedures, and driving insists on relentless attentiveness to motorway codes. Finally, of course, there is the plain truth that an action must be performed at a particular time and at a particular place, and not some other time and place. The future guides and gives shape to freedom and yet does not *determine* what will be the case categorically in every state of affairs. Fixtures of reality persist while their occasioning in time constantly changes—action shapes the future just as future shapes action.

But what do future unknowns mean for the possibilities of action? Is the mystery of what is to come a justifiable reason for indifference? Ferguson's response is offered primarily in section xiv of chapter III, titled "Of a Future State," providing an extended treatment of "man's progressive nature," and takes the following form. First, it outlines what it means for a person to be stationary or progressive and then defines what principles of progression mean for human

---

61. Ibid., 17. Cf. Hume's "Of Suicide," in *Dialogues Concerning Natural Religion*, ed. R. H. Popkin (Indianapolis: Hackett, 1980), 97–105.

nature. Immediately following this brief outline of progress Ferguson takes a more comprehensive look at the nature and function of habituation. This then leads nicely into an engagement with "ambition," or "the desire of something higher than is possessed at present," and goes on to show how habits and ambition contribute to commerce, politics, and fine arts. The chapter then closes its final two sections with "progress in moral apprehension" and "a Future State."

What this movement of thought reveals is Ferguson's view of *how* the future and agent encounter one another. With various habits, aspirations, and pursuits, the dynamic active being confronts the future with powers that the future does not itself possess, while the future confronts the active being with exhortation and mediation. With its regular opportunistic charm, the future encourages action by communicating what kinds of action may or may not contribute to the Good. Man's nature, even if progressive, cannot be relieved of the moral obligation to offer distinct goods to the world. If habits or ambitions do not pursue moral objects, they are evil and altogether blameworthy. Actions either negate the good or affirm it—neutrality is impossible. Indifference, too, is impossible. Habits harness passionate excess, but the final goal of habit is not to eliminate passion or cultivate indifference. Habits *order* passion.

This idea explains why Ferguson condemns only personally or socially corrupting ambitions; ambitions that reach for excellence will not likely be found wrongful. Dr. Johnson's rather general definition for "ambition" as the "desire of something higher than is possessed at present" represents for Ferguson a future of ardent participation in the life of God. When applied to moral understanding ("apprehension"), ambition draws active being toward the resources meant to foster rightful conduct. "To know himself, and his place in the system of nature, is the specific lot and prerogative of man," insists Ferguson, but can only be acquired by actively pursuing this prerogative.[62] Indifference to the future would be for man a moral nemesis, a defeater to the good life manifest in future possibilities.

Hutcheson's assertion that future happiness awaits the completion of acts, in all its utilitarian splendor, dislodges happiness from the act itself and segregates it to consequences the act intended to bring about.[63] Ferguson, of course, argues to the contrary. Happiness and order belong to the action itself, not to consequences that follow performance. The consequences of an action are not within the actor's control, and many are set in motion unintentionally.

62. See "Of the Progress of Moral Apprehension," part I, ch. 3, sect. xiii (306).
63. Hutcheson, *Inquiry*, II.3.

The possibility of future happiness rests not in consequences, but in *hope* inherent to action itself.[64] Futurity reveals opportunities for action while simultaneously blinding us to what the actions may ultimately accomplish. Each active being places hope in what the future may allow and trusts that what is *presently* known and demanded can in fact be acted upon. "To man, the proper subjects of knowledge are the present or the past: Yet, in some instances, the knowledge of these is a knowledge of the future also."[65] This is the will of God, concludes Ferguson, "that man should attend to his present task, and not suffer himself to be diverted from it by prospects of futurity, towards which he can contribute nothing, besides the faithful and diligent performance of a part which is now assigned to him."[66] The axiom for man's future is *Hoc age*, to "mind what you are about."[67] Providence invites one to mind what one is about and leave the future to One who rules eternal.

In recent decades it has become popular to characterize Ferguson as the Scottish Stoic reaching back into antiquity to remind fellow patriots of a national glory once idyllically embodied by Rome.[68] This reading is drawn mainly from isolated readings of specific texts and remains inattentive to the wider unity of his thought. Ferguson is at best a *partial* Stoic. Certain Stoic references appear throughout his writings, of course, but these instances must be integrated into Ferguson's overall world-picture and situated on the hierarchy of his intellectual priorities. As it pertains to active being, moreover, what is of greatest interest to us is the degree to which Ferguson adopts, modifies, or altogether departs from a characteristically Stoic ethic. Stoicism has its own untidy history, as is well known, and in the hands of readers centuries removed it has been forced to take a variety of uncomfortable positions, but untidiness aside, a constructive description of Stoic action theory would help better contextualize Ferguson's reception of it.

First, the nature of human desire in ancient Stoic literature only makes sense as an article of action. Apart from action, the contemplation of desire

64. Robert Spaemann's fascinating treatment of "equanimity," which he defines as "the attitude of someone who regards what he cannot change as a meaningful limit to his ability to act and who accepts this limit," appears congruous to the account provided here by Ferguson. See *Basic Moral Concepts* (London: Routledge, 1989), 85.

65. *Principles*, 319.

66. Ibid., 318.

67. Ibid.

68. For slightly different views on the same interpretation of Ferguson as Stoic, see Jane Fagg, *Adam Ferguson: Scottish Cato* (Chapel Hill: University of North Carolina Press, 1968), and David Kettler, *The Social and Political Thought of Adam Ferguson* (Columbus: Ohio State University Press, 1965).

is purely superfluous. Given this Stoic starting point, one's aspirations are to become personally indifferent to desires that impinge human capacity. When faced with a fixed future the best one can do is become unresponsive to life's narrowing pressures. Desire management makes it humanly possible to then perform all actions, no matter how difficult or anxious, with "fittedness." The Roman Stoic Cicero indicates there are no less than three types of action: virtuous actions, vicious actions, and *intermediates*, that is, actions fitting or unfitting.[69] Whether his view presents the most philosophically exacting version of Stoic action is at this juncture immaterial, what interests us is this property of "fittedness."

Kathekon, often rendered "appropriate" or "befitting" action by modern translators, was conceived as *officium* by Cicero and thus in its transition from Greek to Latin contained a subtle conceptual alteration from the generic impression an action makes on the texture of reality to the "service" or "reasonable duty" one has to one's society. In this way, the meaning of the idea *kathekon* was diversified even at its inception. Cicero's bringing political specificity to fitting action does not alter the way an action should be performed: action should exhibit "rightness" in its performance regardless of whether the action carries political implications. To say that actions must conform to a standard of rightness—or right*eous*ness—is to draw upon language alerting us to limitations, boundaries, and standards. For an action to be capable of achieving rightness it must be equally capable of achieving wrongness, and this differentiation implies a preexisting criterion for judgment. Action is defined as much by the reality in which it is performed as by the resources devoted to its execution. Reality, on the other hand, will disclose what can possibly be accomplished as well as how what *can* be done *could* be done. From a purely physical point of view, for an agent to perform an action in reality means that the subject can by definition do *some*thing but cannot do *any*thing. For the Stoic this is equally true from the moral point of view, given that physical reality shapes definitively what *should* in fact be done.

---

69. Cicero, *Academica Posteriora*, Loeb Classical Library (London: Heinemann, 1913) book I, ch. 37. The appropriateness or inappropriateness of an action, moreover, can emerge only from the circumstantial context from which the action arises and to which the action must respond. The shape of any action's circumstantial fit should not be confused with modern Stoic revivalists, e.g., Kant, and the idea that duties are "categorical." Elsewhere, in *De Officiis*, Cicero seems to have understood *Kathekon* in terms of "ordinary"—in the sense of not "absolute"—duty, which must be reasonably justified. Both absolute and ordinary duties carry political import, but with varying degrees. See Loeb translation by W. Miller (London: Heinemann, 1913), 1.3.8.

Coming to an understanding of reality imposes moral obligations that only *reason* can adjudicate. J. M. Rist has summed up this reason-reality interface by explaining that "in the Stoic world there is only one thing which can be called good without any qualification whatsoever . . . the providentially ordered life in accordance with reason."[70] The good to be achieved through action evades immediate understanding. Goodness, particularly the good to be achieved by action, first requires recognition—*katalepsis*—then contemplation. Prior to action one must give deliberate reflection both to what should be done, as well as to how that dutiful action might best be carried out. This is a critical feature of the Stoic account of action: intentionality is not the *sole* determinant of an action's moral goodness because each such action must also be performed with a measure of excellence. Put in these terms, the reasons for describing action as either affirming truth or careening into falsity become decisive. To have performed an action truthfully is to have dealt rightly with reality—to have recognized how to do what is right. For the Stoic, truth and goodness hold transcendent jurisdiction over the realm of subjects in nature; they cannot be comprehensively defined and yet cannot be overlooked. Cicero depicts this narrative of moral learning as man's attempt to bring action into "conformity" with the goods of reality, that is, with the goods of nature as presented in reality itself. In *homologia* ("conformity") "resides that Good which is the End to which all else is a means, moral conduct and Moral Worth itself, which alone is counted good . . . and is nevertheless the sole thing that is for its own efficacy and value desirable."[71]

Before concluding our treatment of Ferguson's partial Stoicism it would be useful to comment on two additional Stoic concepts. First, it is everywhere assumed in Stoic literature that only virtue is good in itself. Action on this view is merely the outcome or result of a particular quality of virtue. But is it really the case that only virtue can be good in itself? Could not action, too, be considered a true good? The trouble with vesting goodness squarely in virtue is that virtue is itself formed by a particular excellence of action. Acquiring virtue is consequent upon the nature of an action already conducted; that is, by doing good deeds and thereby becoming good. "Repetition of the right action will forward the development of a right concept (*ennoia*) in the soul."[72] Hume referred to similar formations as "habituation." Either way, it is not in *passivity*

---

70. J. M. Rist, *Stoic Philosophy* (Cambridge: Cambridge University Press, 1969), 13.

71. Cicero, *De Finibus*, Loeb Classical Library (London: Heinemann, 1913), book III, ch. 21.

72. *Stoic Philosophy*, 14.

that virtue is acquired, but in *activity*. Virtue alone cannot be called good in itself.

The second lingering concept, on the other hand, has a less direct bearing on a Stoic understanding of action. How is action to be understood when the external determinations impressed on action by the laws of reality lay wholly outside one's control? In bringing this question to the fore we have come around full circle: it was with the abolition of desire that this treatment of Stoicism began. The rationale for eliminating desire, as is well known, emboldens individuals to face down the unknowns of future affairs with fortitude and temperance. Such future states of affairs will somewhat paradoxically include a subject's own contributions to an approaching reality already entirely predetermined. *Kathekon*, then, is the best one can do when certain consequences are erased from the content of action and the wise man is all that remains: "For the Stoic view is that happiness, which means life in harmony with nature, is a matter of seizing the right moment. So that Wisdom her very self upon occasion bids the Wise Man to leave her."[73]

ARTISTRY, COMMUNICATION, AND TRANSTEMPORALITY IN COMMERCE

Notice the language Ferguson uses to describe properties of active being and the reality onto which actions make their mark: the language of "good" and "evil" triumphs over the use of "happy" and "miserable"; the language of "right" and "wrong" takes precedent over "approbation" and "disapprobation"; and the mind-body dualism presumed throughout the *Principles* places him in direct contrast to Humean reductions.[74] Man is both partially free and partially determined; he acts and is acted upon; he is autonomous and yet is necessarily social. Creator and created, ruler and ruled, active being and passive being are all tensions to which Ferguson gives repeated reference. The "unity of being" so revered by Stoicism is for Ferguson the direct result of man's participation in the work of providence:

[T]he highest point to which moral science conducts the mind of man, is that eminence of thought, from which he can view himself as but a part in the community of living natures; by which he is in

73. *De Finibus*, book III, ch. 63.

74. The language of "happy" or "miserable" and "approbation" or "disapprobation" is most directly applicable to Smith's *Theory of Moral Sentiments*, which is, as the title indicates, essentially a sentimentalization of ethical theory.

some measure let into the design by God, to combine all the parts together for the common benefit of all; and can state himself as a willing instrument for this purpose, in what depends on his own will; and as a conscious instrument, at the disposal of providence, in matters which are out of his power.[75]

This notion of agency as *instrumental* participation in the life of God is how the Christian tradition has characteristically conceived of its mission. St. Paul's instruction on Christian action, for example, illustrates the point rather well: one is to fulfill their particular calling in the wider body of Christ (1 Corinthians 12); offer oneself as a living sacrifice (Rom. 12:1); and put on the new man while sloughing off the old (Col. 3:9-10). Each metaphor represents for Paul an active, albeit submissive, participation in the life of God that is always secondarily for the church and common good. The unity of being coheres in God. The word used by St. Paul to refer to action—*praxis*—is used sparingly in his letters. He is more inclined to use *energeia*, often translated as "labor," or "striving." This particular term, from which moderns have derived the word "energy," implies a degree of *effort*, an exerting of one's powers for achieving objectives.[76] For God's part, paradoxically, this *energeia* is effortless; an efficacious operation performed by God within the individual.[77] God acts in us so that we may act in him; a participatory life St. Paul compares to "offering oneself as a living sacrifice" and "walking in the Spirit."[78] Active movement into God's own activities means the disciple has "stripped off old behavior" and his "old self," and has "put on a new self which will progress towards true knowledge the more it is renewed in the image of its creator" (Col. 3:9-10). What is at the center of this "true knowledge"? "There is only Christ: he is everything and he is in everything" (Col. 3:11).

In conjunction with the language of "newness," Paul concurrently utilizes the political and juridical language of "obedience," "submission," "charity," and "justice." Indeed, the letter to the Romans is in many respects a jurisprudential, political elaboration of the gospel message. For Paul, the task of each citizen is to observe and strictly adhere to the law (lowercase "l"), submit to the authorities, and love one's neighbor as oneself. The jurist in Paul conceives of

---

75. *Principles*, 313.

76. This "exertion" is put forth predominantly by God and secondarily by man, but is also occasionally effected by impersonal forces such as sin, death, and the word.

77. A few examples, for which there are many, include: 1 Cor. 12:6; Phil. 2:13; Col. 2:12; Eph. 1:11, 19-20.

78. Rom. 12:1; Gal. 5:13-26.

life as an ordered totality for whom "to live is Christ," the essence of order, truth, and goodness. The "fitting" life for man is to become the "bond-slave" of Christ and submit steadfastly to his absolute authority. The object of life therefore is to align oneself obediently with the good as expressed and ordered by his rule. And although Paul is being taken only as an example from the Christian tradition, this configuration is strangely resonant with Ferguson's vision for active being. "Putting on the new man" complements Ferguson's reflections on moral ambition and the striving for excellence; to submit to the law is to obediently perform actions "fitting" the shape of obligation; juridical and "energetic" languages are used routinely and interchangeably by Ferguson throughout his written corpus. A brief overview of three overarching themes will strengthen the connection I am attempting to draw between Ferguson's theory of action and his Christian commitments, which for the sake of clarity will be broadly labeled: Art, Communication, and Time.

In both his *Essay* and *Principles*, Ferguson refers repeatedly to the practice of "art." All action must exhibit a degree of excellence and should therefore be performed *artistically*. To perform an action with artistry is to perform a deliberate—in the sense of "deliberation," not the truncated, late-modern "intentionality"—action excellently and with a definite good as one's principal object. In other words, the action must be properly deliberated, masterfully performed, and carried out in such a way that it contributes both to the common good and to the good of God's kingdom. "[I]t is in the wisdom of God, not the deliberate effect of invention or choice, which the created being is fitted to employ for himself . . . [that] his task is *prescribed* and his manner of performing it secured."[79] The best one can do is give every effort to the task God assigns, to take up one's work with an artistry exuding gratitude and striving for imitation. For "[m]an is formed for an *artist*; and he must be allowed, even when he mistakes the purpose of his work, to practice his calling, in order to find out for himself what is best for him to perform."[80]

In addition to owning artistic quality, actions should also communicate on each performance. Since one comes to understand how to act artistically from those who have come before, actions communicate primarily through the institution of custom, disclosing and forming personal character simultaneously. Past actions communicate with the future through the megaphone of the present. Creation is configured in such a way that "[t]he chain of communication extends from one to many, from species to species, and even

---

79. Ibid., 53.
80. Ibid., 299.

from world to world, throughout the intellectual as well as material system of nature."[81] Actions artistically performed, therefore, are a type of noiseless speech directed toward the community into which the action was undertaken and unto the God who oversees every exertive enterprise no matter how trivial. "Arts *communicate*," suggests Ferguson, "by information and example, from the master to his pupil, and from a passing generation to that which succeeds it; so that the progress of the human species is not, like that of other animals, limited to the individual or to the age; but communicated from one to another, and continued from age to age."[82] The content of meaningful action accumulates with each and every inheritance. A new age receives from the old a body of instruction that takes aim at an everlasting target. The idea, as is stressed throughout biblical literature, is to make contributions that do not perish but are chronicled in the listless volumes of public memory. Positive or negative, virtuous or vicious, praiseworthy or blameworthy, what ultimately comes of an action cannot be controlled and thus the certitude surrounding its achievements released. The aim of artistic action is simply to give something of charitable endurance to the world.

Lastly, artistry and communication partner cooperatively in the encompassing and nurturing arms of time. Every action performed with artistry communicates, and every communication brings together past, present, and future so that all three moments are made one in the unifying power of active being. Action makes the present feel existentially real by maintaining a contiguous vision of the future and past, creating "moments" in which time's passage is "presented." The fleeting character of the present is only temporarily overcome when action takes the past in one hand, the future in the other hand, and combines them into an ontological present. Action is to a large degree transtemporal and yet it alone leaves a mark on the temporal realm. To act faithfully is to act simultaneously in *and* upon time, explaining *why* every action should be artistic and communicative. "Men are equally engaged by the past, the present, and the future," suggests Ferguson, "and are prepared for every occupation that gives scope to their powers."[83]

But what brings ultimate unity to artistic actions communicated in and across time? For Ferguson, the answer is God. "The past, the present, and the future are but one object to the supreme intelligence of *God*, why not also to the created mind, so far as it is qualified to partake in this view of things, and can delight in contemplating the effects of eternal beneficence, whether

81. *Principles*, vol. II, 324.
82. Ibid., 175 (emphasis mine).
83. *Principles*, vol. I, 164.

past, present, or to come?"[84] It is from God that one receives the wisdom necessary to conduct an act artistically; it is by the power of God that actions are communicated in and upon time; and it is because God himself actively communicates with his children in time that humanity itself is empowered to act and communicate. Artistic communication in and across time is an *identical imitation of how God himself acts*. Ferguson can therefore emphatically affirm Paul's declaration that God "is everything and is in everything"—our "all in all." All good and truthful action is *imitatio Dei*; a righteous performance "by, in, and for" the God whose creative artistry communicates responsively with mankind in and over time. His creative communication actualizes goods through the use of his "instruments"—his people—to perpetuate order and meet human needs. In acting righteously one trusts that God is in and behind the act, bringing about the very best that action can possibly bring about.[85] The meaning of action is disclosed in the riches of history; it "discovers" a meaning, as Ferguson has told us, and ultimately comes to mean what Providence decides. Action is taken up into the caring arms of the *Alpha* and *Omega* of active being.

The significance of Ferguson's active triad—artistic, communicative, and transtemporal—is perhaps nowhere better illustrated than by its application to the commercial sphere. The commercial order, such as it existed in Ferguson's time, was in many respects still an artisan culture. Occupations were usually dictated to individuals by circumstances lying entirely outside their control; birth order, family rank, political conflict, and agricultural stability name only a few such exigencies. Nearly all professions, whether of statesman, farmer, mason, or trader, required an element of *craftsmanship*. Each profession was mutually dependent upon the other and so how well one performed their trade was crucial to their continued subsistence and reputation. Prudence applied to one's occupation best serves the community and satisfies one's own familial needs. For the tradesman of eighteenth-century Scotland, craftsmanship was the defining virtue of actions directed to commercial ends.

In an age where members of Western societies are pressed to direct all energies toward commercial outlets, it is difficult to imagine a world in which one's economic actions would be judged precisely *by* their quality. The decisive question for our purposes is whether something vitally important has been lost.

---

84. Ibid., 335.

85. Along similar lines, Robert Spaemann has remarked that religion is "characterized by the fact that it sees both [the success and failure of action] as having the same cause. On the one hand God is seen as the source and guarantor of moral obligation. On the other hand He is seen as the Lord of History; that is to say that He is still honored even if our good intentions fail, and, what is more, He is seen as the guarantee that good intentions will ultimately be reconciled with the course of history."

Is it at all strange that to be an "artist" in the late-modern world is, as it were, to occupy a sanctified category of almost pitiable *in*activity in the truest sense of the word? Why has the artistic quality of commercial labors been lost? Without answering a question that will be taken up more explicitly in the next chapter, it is sufficient here to hint at the abstract and highly individualized character of contemporary economic models. The actual tasks that one undertakes in today's economy are dissolved into the unrelenting and ever-retreating goals of capital acquisition, which sweeps up into its forceful progress all labor and translates it into "liquidity." The economy's enormous growth has reduced labor to a mechanical function where one's "employment" typically takes the form of turning knobs, pulling levers, or clicking buttons. It goes without saying, perhaps, that there are certain creative limits to organizing spreadsheets.

The virtual abstraction characteristic of modern economy also negatively affects how commercial actions are communicated. On Ferguson's account, good and truthful actions are performed unto God and neighbor. In eighteenth-century Edinburgh, normal exchanges between different members of society were conducted on familiar terms—one knew their partner in exchange, their produce and reputation, and that was why they did business together. A neighbor was someone known in friendship or trust. Such a level of familiarity is almost impossible to achieve in contemporary economies, since the person or persons with whom one does business are unlikely to be persons at all, but a collection of invisible shareholders, or worse, an electronic program behind a corporate brand. But this perplexing situation, which admittedly some workers do not see as perplexing in the slightest but simply "the way things are," arises out of a logically prior quandary involving conferral of market goods and labor. Perhaps the most demeaning implication of modern labor's continued mutation from craft to function in Western economies is the fact that one's labors seem quite literally to go nowhere and contribute nothing. Enormous amounts of human energy are devoted to labors already destined for absorption into the market machine—processed and squeezed for every drop of value. Who exactly does this taking, processing, and squeezing cannot be identified with great specificity, of course, because it remains largely unclear what *real* thing is being contributed. When an office administrator circulates memos, answers telephones, and photocopies reports, for example, *where*, exactly, does the labor go? What is the character of their contribution? How are those who never interact with physical objects—minus computational devices, of course, since that is the only means for "producing" in an economy disenchanted with physical matter—to understand their place or involvement in the wider "business model"? Such questions allude to the onerous dilemma of being personally unaware of how one fits within the economic order or of how one's commercial activities communicatewith others. If one of my neighbors is a systems analyst and the other neighbor a Web technician, how or what do their actions communicate in the marketplace, if they deliver any content at all?

For Ferguson, it is clear that when one submits oneself as an instrument to God's purposes, every action so conducted becomes a candidate for transtemporal endurance. Given the tendency of modern economy to minimize artistic, communicative action from the commercial sphere, the question to be put to the modern economist is: How can one act in today's economy *for* God and his kingdom? When a job is by all intents and purposes completely arbitrary, or could just as easily be left undone, how is one to consider one's work a legitimate contribution, much less an *eternal* one? Every member of society wishes to leave behind something permanent and enduring, something that can be given as a gift to one's neighbors and to generations still to come. Under contemporary economic circumstances, however, there is little way of knowing what, exactly, one's commercial actions realistically accomplish, and therefore everyone's attempt to leave something behind is surrendered to forces beyond their control. The market machine itself now confuses between the kinds of commercial action that truly last and those that merely generate capital. If an action lives on, it will do so in the form of fiscal liquidity and eventually find its way into unimagined pockets.

4

The Peril of Commercial Society

If ultimately we wish to understand why the specific brand of democratic capitalism we late-moderns have inherited appears to create and intensify political disorder, if we detect a problem in the present configuration of the marketplace, how then has the problem of disorder arisen? In what way do the political and economic spheres relate to one another? How do the controls and commitments of market ideology become systemically embedded in political structures? Questions like these are responded to insightfully by Ferguson, and his perceiving moral and political problems so early in the genesis of capitalism helps underscore the observation that even in its beginning, its ends were often contradictory.

Responding to this question of how certain economic institutions and practices compromise the political architecture of Western modernity requires a slight methodological turn. This essay will broaden the Fergusonian portrait by sketching his account of a morally and politically subservient commercial order. We will begin, perhaps unexpectedly, with his advocacy for the establishment of local militias, which affords useful insight into his martial emphases and makes the rationale for his Principle of Defense more pronounced. With the militia issue in mind we will then carefully rehearse the movement of Ferguson's argument as presented in the *Essay on the History of Civil Society*. Here we are determined to make the historical and moral character of his political thought as clear as possible. The history of civil society discloses unique patterns and developments, continuities and discontinuities, helping us diagnose how and why history experiences transitions as it does. Ferguson narrates for us a misfortune that has occurred previously in the history of society and will likely occur again. Grasping the historical texture of the story will allow us to proceed at last to the moment of methodological shift where application of his argument to contemporary Western societies will be most suitable. It will be particularly important at this stage to resist venturing into wild abstractions; and to avoid the temptation of wandering into the no-man's land of theoretical economic "modeling," concrete examples will be incorporated to illustrate the astuteness of Ferguson's account and highlight the extent to which commercial forces have usurped undue control of political institutions. On final pass it will be clear how this deposition has occurred and what the moral significance of this change might be for dis-integrated capitalist societies.

The Militia Issue

Even after his honorable discharge, Ferguson's military service never really concluded. He spoke fondly, even romantically of his military service because that is how he conceived of it—as *service*. To be a military man required submission to an exceptional class of discipline, order, masculine virtue, and honor; military service epitomized a civic service above which no higher display could be achieved. In this regard Ferguson's loyalties lay decisively with Great Britain, which were what decided his assignment to the Black Watch in the first place and was later doubly confirmed by his *Sermon in Ersh Language*.[1] Roughly ten years later and well into his retirement from active duty he published the mildly contentious pamphlet, *Reflections Previous to the Establishment of a Militia*.[2] His principal argument that militia service makes a positive contribution to civil society and affords the enlisted an opportunity to exercise virtues of courage and self-discipline held much to the classical line. "Self-defense is the business of all," he insists, and to establish a successful local militia two things are required: that rotating members of the militia familiarize themselves with weaponry, and an order of authority be instituted for the "habit of military obedience."[3] Standard objections to militias are then recited and quickly dismissed with underdeveloped, if not wholly inadequate rebuttals.

Or so it would seem. Perhaps the better reason for his use of weaker or near-impotent responses to his critics is that *Reflections* primarily addresses establishment of militias and the benefits they bestow upon civic virtues and to local defense, and in doing so reveals along the way to its conclusion a

---

1. Matthew Arbo, "Adam Ferguson's *Sermon in the Ersh Language*: A Word from 2 Samuel on Martial Responsibility and Political Order," *Political Theology* 12, no. 6 (2011): 894–908.

2. Adam Ferguson, *Reflections Previous to the Establishment of a Militia* (London: R. & J. Dodsley, 1756).

3. Ibid., 20. On this and other subjects, especially the ownership and use of arms, Ferguson is perhaps indebted to Machiavelli's *Prince* (Cambridge: Cambridge University Press, 1998) and to Harrington's *The Commonwealth of Oceana* (Cambridge: Cambridge University Press, 1992).

deep suspicion harbored toward the maintenance of permanent standing armies. He supports militias, but not nearly as much as he opposes the expense and potential tyranny of standing armies. This is precisely why his response to objections in the pamphlet comes across as muted; the establishment of purely defensive militias is a lesser evil than the tyrannical threat of a standing army. The argument could not have been put more cautiously.

On this issue Ferguson stands within an interesting tradition of Scottish political suspicion. Nearly sixty years prior, the able parliamentarian and political theorist Andrew Fletcher of Saltoun had also proposed the establishment of militias, and with more constructive detail. Fletcher explained how, in his own time, "most princes of Europe are in possession of the sword by standing mercenary forces kept up in time of peace, absolutely depending upon them," and how "all such governments are changed from monarchies to tyrannies."[4] Maintaining standing armies was the ultimate error of the Roman Empire, which on Fletcher's account represents the fall of antiquity's last great standing army. From the gradual division of the Roman Empire arose a network of territories governed by kings, subdivided for barons, and then subdivided again for vassals; everyone had access to productive property or had at least secured general means of subsistence. By the turn of the eighteenth century, however, the economy's adverse effects were wearing this conception of militarism ruinously thin. "The only remaining security we have," complained Fletcher, "is that no standing armies were ever yet allowed in time of peace, the parliament of England having so often and so expressly declared them to be contrary to law."[5]

The 1689 Bill of Rights had set preventative measures that no standing army could be maintained without the express consent of parliament. By Fletcher's lights this "consent" was being rudely stretched and it seemed only a matter of time before these measures were perceived as all but unbinding ceremony. In truth, *power* is the fulcrum of politics. To give the monarch a standing army "puts his power beyond control, and consequently makes him absolute."[6] The sword constitutes the true force behind political will and the bitter tip of its authority. When tyranny quickens, little protects the populace from a monarch's sprawling controls, for, as J. G. Pocock has commented, "once armies were paid for by taxes, taxes were collected by armies and the liberties of nearly all Europe were at an end."[7] Still worse, one can assume any ruler

---

4. Andrew Fletcher, "A Discourse of Government with Relation to Militias," in *Political Works*, ed. John Robertson (Cambridge: Cambridge University Press, 1997), 3.

5. Ibid., 19.

6. Ibid.

thus empowered will turn readily to conquest. But "conquest is not in our interest," insisted Fletcher, because it consumes both life and treasure—the very things that conquests are meant to improve—with deplorable alacrity.[8] Tyranny expresses itself domestically as a suppression of personal and public freedoms, and internationally as a deleterious program for conquest. Establishing a standing army would therefore mean the beginning of national enslavement and explains why "a good militia is of such importance to a nation."[9]

For Ferguson the problem is slightly more nuanced. Maintenance of standing armies may imply certain irrecoverable political compromises, but more troublesome by far is the negative impact a loss of civic participation might have on the moral character of individual agents, and by extension to civil society itself. Societies unexercised in armed conflict are prone to alien domination as they prove themselves devoid of virtues necessary *to defend the cities of their God*.[10] The martially unprepared are never genuinely free. Several years later when Ferguson expanded his lectures, published as *Principles of Moral and Political Science*, in a section on the meaning of political liberty he takes aim at the doctrinaire classification of liberty as an "absence of restraint," defining it instead as "the operation of just government and the exemption from injury of any sort, rather than merely an exemption from restraint; for it actually implies every just restraint."[11] Freedom is not gained by jettisoning restraints but by implementing and actively enforcing *just* restraints. Conceptually, freedom implies protective measures. So important is the protective impetus of freedom that "security, in fact, is the essence of freedom, and if security is to be obtained under political establishment alone, there also is freedom obtained."[12] Freedom and security belong to one another.

In rejecting the idea of liberty realized by the absence of restraint, he also rejects the notion of freedom consisting in equality of station or rank. The trouble with fusing liberty and equality, he thinks, is "individuals are destined to inequality from their birth," which then leads naturally to "all the varieties of possession and fortune."[13] Moreover, "the only respect in which all men continue forever to be equal is that of the equal right which every man has to defend himself," although this clearly admits an inequality in the things to be

7. J. G. A. Pocock, *The Machiavellian Moment* (Princeton: Princeton University Press, 1975), 430.

8. Ibid., 30.

9. Ibid., 21.

10. Arbo, "Adam Ferguson's *Sermon in the Ersh Language*."

11. Adam Ferguson, *Principles of Moral and Political Science* (New York: Garland, 1978), 459.

12. Ibid., 461.

13. Ibid., 462.

defended.[14] Defense of person and property is the only equity. The conditions of society may become unequal, even grossly so, but "it is impossible to prevent the inequality of condition in the fortunes of men without violating the first and common principles of right in the most flagrant manner."[15] For government to force equality upon a people is to violate the basic right to defend one's person and property. Therefore, on Ferguson's account, equality cannot serve as a principle of justice.

Only the Principle of Security rightly prioritizes liberty and equality, and helps to explain why militias remain an urgent necessity. The aim of the state should be to establish the conditions within which freedom can flourish, not to impose impossible ideals coercively upon an impervious people. We will see later why Ferguson believes democracy cannot serve as a principle of freedom either. For now, it is enough simply to identify the vitality of militias in his political theory. Militias ensure that society is defended and that the bluntest instrument of modern coercive power is decentralized.

Ferguson's Principle of Defense has direct relevance to the moral question of war-making itself. He makes able use of Hugo Grotius' principles of just war to support his conviction that nations should take a natural posture of defense, not of aggression, in matters of international conflict.[16] Conquest, the domination of another territory for reasons of interest, is not a sufficient condition for the declaration of war, and neither should war be waged on the supposition of fear or potential animosities. War is almost wholly reactive; "the success of arms cannot change wrong into right, and . . . any supposed right of conquest arising from the success of a war is a mere solecism in language and the reverse of any just tenet of natural law."[17] The political reality is that "nations are . . . almost in every instance mutual objects of jealousy and distrust, and must think themselves safe so far only as they are severely in condition to maintain their respective rights."[18] Yet modern nations, despite mutual jealousy and distrust, should use force only as a "last resort" aimed at "the redress of wrongs."[19] Ferguson's Principle of Defense reaffirms the just war tradition's

14. Ibid.

15. Ibid., 463.

16. Hugo Grotius, *The Rights of War and Peace*, trans. A. C. Campbell (London: M. Walter Dunne, 1901). For Ferguson's interaction with Grotius see part II, chapter iv, section 4 of the *Principles*. Grotius' jurisprudence, according to Ferguson, is "so intermixed with quotations from the custom and practice of different ages, with considerations of duty as well as right, that his work becomes a system of ethics, and the history of opinions and customs, rather than a simple deduction and application of the principles of compulsory law" (295).

17. Ferguson, *Principles*, 312.

18. Ibid., 294.

rebuke of aggressive conquest. His points here and those above on the imperial tendencies of standing armies achieve even greater relevance in his pointed critique of modern commercial society.[20] By the end of my exposition of Ferguson's *Essay* below, the political complications introduced to commercial exchange by martial expansion will have become clear.

Essay on the History of Civil Society

Bearing the subtleties of the militia issue in mind we are now in position to identify the broader logic of Ferguson's argument in the *Essay on the History of Civil Society*. Society is the main character in his story, and its journey down the corridor of commercial advancement constitutes the plotline. As we saw in chapter 2, the history of civil society informs us of our contemporary circumstances by teaching us how to identify problems that have arisen before and respond sensibly to novel challenges. History is a sage. And in response to the commercial incongruities, complexities, and contradictions of modern society, history is Ferguson's preferred guide for exploring the boundaries and forms of commercial life.

Why have human beings always been found joined together in communities large and small? Given what we have discovered in Ferguson's Principle of Defense and theoretical tendencies of eighteenth-century political thought in general, the reader is likely unsurprised by his immediate appeal to self-preservation as a basic principle of social formation. Humans have always been found in companies, and the cause of this assemblage is "the principle of their alliance or union."[21] Human beings are social from beginning, for *it is not good for man to be alone* (Gen. 2:18). Distinguishing between self-love and self-interest is therefore essential to any coherent principle of social union.[22] Interest, we are told, "arises from the principles of self-preservation

---

19. Ibid., 305.

20. Roughly one hundred years later (1876) the British poet and artisan William Morris would object to the government's interest-driven rationale for war with Russia on precisely these grounds, insisting that purveyors of war would deliver its people "bound hand and foot forever to irresponsible capital." This quotation comes from "To the Working Men of England," an unpublished essay referred to but not included in *Political Writings of William Morris*, ed. A. L. Morton (London: Lawrence & Wishart, 1973), 18.

21. Ibid., 21.

22. Examples that blur this distinction, if only taken from the Scottish school, include: Francis Hutcheson, *On Human Nature*, ed. T. Mautner (Cambridge: Cambridge University Press, 1993); Adam Smith, *Theory of Moral Sentiments*, ed. D. D. Raphael and A. L. Macfie (Indianapolis: Liberty Fund, 1982);

in the human frame, but is a corruption, or at least a partial result of those principles, and is upon many accounts very improperly termed *self-love*."[23] Identification of self-interest with self-love is mistaken because "love is an affection which carries the attention of the mind beyond itself, and has a quality which we call tenderness, that never can accompany the considerations of interest."[24] Confusing love with interest leads to deep ambiguities over the affective powers giving rise to political action as such. The idea of interest "commonly implies little more than our regard for property" and in turn complicates social cohesion, but because love is self-transcending by definition Ferguson reckons it essential to the principle of self-preservation itself. That I am taken care of is a consequence of having loved others first, not accidentally loving others by caring chiefly for myself. "Mutual discoveries of generosity, joint trials of fortitude, redouble the ardors of friendship and kindle a flame in the human breast which the considerations of personal interest or safety *cannot* express."[25]

United to this notion of love as self-transcendence is the cooperative overcoming of adversity. "Affection operates with the greatest force where it meets with the greatest difficulties," a force illustrated vividly by the ancient Greeks and Romans, who understood how affections created and nourished bonds of union through allegiance to nation, land, and honor. The ancient citizen thus cuts a striking contrast to the citizen of the modern state:

> Let those examples be compared with the spirit which reigns in a commercial state, where men may be supposed to have experienced, in its full extent, the interest which individuals have in the preservation of their country. It is here indeed, if ever, that man is sometimes found a *detached* and a *solitary being*: he has found an object which sets him in *competition* with his fellow creatures, and he deals with them as he does with his cattle and his soil, *for the sake of the profits they bring*. The mighty engine which we suppose to

David Hume, *Enquiries Concerning Human Understanding*, ed. P. H. Nidditch (Oxford: Clarendon, 1988); *Essays Moral, Political and Literary*, ed. E. F. Miller (Indianapolis: Liberty Fund, 1987).

23. Ferguson, *Essay*, 18.

24. Ibid. We would do well to note in passing that Ferguson avoids the semantic trap so alluring to other eighteenth-century theorists of conflating passions and interests, a theoretical tendency of the period shown clearly by A. O. Hirschman in *The Passions and the Interests* (Princeton: Princeton University Press, 1997). See especially chapter one of this now-famous economic historiography.

25. Ibid., 22 (emphasis mine).

have formed society, only tends to set its members at variance, or to continue their intercourse after the bands of affection are broken.[26]

The duty of all society members is to protect and foster community. "No person is so far insignificant as not to be able, in some particular, to contribute to the welfare of others."[27] Conspicuously absent from Ferguson's account of society is any semblance of voluntarism. Membership in society is not premised upon voluntary consent, but upon one's natural birth, everyone being born into a community and thus given to that community on its terms. "Man is by nature the member of a community, and when considered in this capacity the individual appears to be no longer made for himself."[28] Birth is a blessing to the community and although responsibilities to one's community shift with age, the fundamental duty to serve the needs of others never slackens.

Those who stand *for* the community, patriots for whom ministry to the fatherland is an enriching privilege, remain always tethered by the bonds of neighborly affection. They belong together and they belong where they dwell. This kind of existence, one dis-interested and directed toward the communal good, is characterized by Ferguson as a Savage existence. He has in mind the native tribes of North America with their unpropertied and yet naturally stratified social order. The savage's egalitarian occupations are simple: to contribute to the subsistence of the tribe and to help defend it as necessary—everyone occupies a definite role and place. The prospect of physical challenge is all that excites them. These savages enjoy an admirable existence devoid of greed or acquisitiveness. Throughout the *Essay* he refers to savages, and later to barbarians, as a "rude" people. He means "rude" in the sense of "coarse" or "unrefined," but whereas many of his contemporaries portray savages and barbarians in a mockingly primitive light, he uses them to illustrate how well a society can be ordered when property and wealth acquisition are not its dominant concerns. The irony with which he employs the savage as a literary tool will be seen more clearly later; for now, it is sufficient to note that the primitive political condition of the savage is linked to their lack of property and indifference to wealth. For those members of modern society who do not view themselves as *for* the community, on the other hand, personal pursuits become detached and self-directed. Members of society addicted to self-interest quickly begin to treat others as useful to their aims. No longer are they the object of pursuit, but instead become the means to other, less honorable ends.

---

26. Ibid., 24 (emphasis mine).
27. Ibid., 247.
28. Ibid., 59.

With the introduction of private property into civil society's history a revolutionary conversion takes place. Savages and Barbarians either could not conceive of possessing land or else did not value it to the point of rampant accumulation. Their disinterestedness implies that "rude" peoples, because they did not hold property, "admit of no distinctions of rank or condition, and they have in fact no degree of subordination different from the distribution of function."[29] Property possession inaugurates an alternative configuration to the political hierarchy. The power of property changes the essential *criteria* of authority, because "where no profit attends dominion, one party is as much averse to the trouble of perpetual command as the other is to the mortification of perpetual submission."[30] In other words, political power is no longer natural, but artificial and coerced. Savages, like those of North America, are constituted by affections of equitable friendship and kindness, whereas the modern European it seems would "rather corrupt than improve the system of morality" by making repeated "demands for attention."[31] The savages conceive of authority in terms of individual capacity, moderns in terms of possession. Characteristic of savages is a pervasive sense of contentment, disinterest in wealth, and commitment to testing fortitude. Political conditions for the savage appear always conducive to friendship. Indebtedness, the reality upon which modern commerce is founded, compromises genuine friendship by leveraging one neighbor against another and sinking the relationship into pure compensatory contract.

In addition to reshaping criteria of authority and fracturing bonds of friendship, the establishment of property can also tarnish personal freedom and interest. The sight of another's acquisition initially motivates one to acquire property for oneself in fear that putting if off might lead to serious deprivations. This sense of fear, coupled with jealousies arising later, provokes members to amass their own resources and hoard them away. The change is essentially one of perspective: from "What can I do to assist my neighbor?" to "How am I going to take care of myself?" The idea of private property made this transition possible. Something has come between my neighbor and me demanding close and constant attention, and which inverts the orientation of our friendship.

Next, "the individual having now a *separate interest*, the bands of society must become less firm and domestic disorders more frequent."[32] This is what we might call "step one" in the loosening of social cohesion. Property reminds

---

29. Ibid., 83.
30. Ibid.
31. Ibid., 87.
32. Ibid., 97 (emphasis mine).

us over and again that we have *interests* needful of protection and promotion, and once this cycle of acquisition has commenced it accelerates at astonishing speed. At some point in history this acceleration led even to the consecration of a monarch who had allocated enough property to rule all surrounding territories at will. According to Ferguson, this historical development from mere possession of property to the consecration of monarchs illustrates how *fortune* operates to establish rank and social status: "When the distinctions of fortune and those of birth are conjoined," society is almost permanently stratified—subordinates find their purpose in the glory of the monarch and are even "guided by his smiles and his frowns."[33] Possession of wealth and the political status accompanying it become more or less customary and eventually gain legal support—tradition reinforces perception. At this juncture the concepts of property and interest converge to the confusion of both:

> It is in this woeful condition that mankind, being slavish, interested, insidious, deceitful, and bloody, bear marks, if not of the least curable, surely of the most lamentable sort of *corruption*. Among them, war is the mere practice of rapine to enrich the individual; commerce is turned into a system of snares and impositions, and government turns oppressive or weak.[34]

Property and interest seem therefore to reinforce one another—property becomes an interest and interests concentrate on property.

It would be useful at this juncture to pause a moment and consider Ferguson's theory of right and critique of ideal liberty. In a section titled, "Of the Political Arts," a theory for reasonable political engagement is propounded. The causes of injustice are not located in the legal or authorial parameters of the political institutions themselves or the constitutional foundation of society, but in "the collision of private interests and passions; or from the interfering of private with public concerns."[35] Frictions generated by competing interests test the ability of government to remedy disparate claims. At one moment it guards against abuses, and the next it checks the proportion of its own abuses. The state is not privileged with omniscience or omnipotence and so it must make do with what resources it has at its disposal at the time. Some form of political art is therefore needed to achieve lasting civic order.

33. Ibid., 99.

34. Ibid., 101 (emphasis mine).

35. Ferguson, *Principles*, 261.

The question, of course, is what the *right* means for doing so might be, and in response Ferguson appeals to Grotian jurisprudence.[36] The term *right* is defined as "the relation of a person to a thing in which no alteration ought to be made, without his own consent."[37] Right is objective and expresses the qualitative relation between things. Violation of right is a *wrong*. And thus the task of every citizen "is not to give society existence . . . but to perfect the society in which he finds himself already by nature placed; not to establish subordination, but to correct the *abuse* of a subordination already established."[38] Political arts renew society through the righting of divisive, self-interested wrongs. One might even call the work of political arts *redemptive*: "Society, in which alone the distinctions of right and wrong are exemplified, may be considered as the garden of God, in which the tree of knowledge of good and evil is planted; and in which men are destined to distinguish, and to choose, among its fruits."[39]

But lest one be misled, individual liberty likewise is right only in a particular, not absolute sense. Zealots of liberty have historically encountered all varieties of disorder, "and adventurers under pretence of promoting it, have found their way to the most violent and pernicious usurpations."[40] Exemplary evils of the French Revolution come swiftly to mind, and seeing as how the *Principles* were not published until 1792, perhaps it is one such "pernicious usurpation" Ferguson bears in mind. His philosophical approach to liberty is arrived at by way of negation, naming what liberty does *not* consist in. First, "Liberty . . . is not, as the origin of the name may seem to imply, an exemption from all restraint; but, rather, the most effectual application of every just restraint to all the members of a free state, whether they be magistrates or subjects."[41] Freedom must resonate with justice. Second, liberty cannot consist in equal station or fortune. Equality has not existed since the fall of humanity, and regardless of whether one insists on an equality of possession or of capacity, both are misguided:

---

36. For an excellent elucidation of Grotius' theory of right, see Oliver O'Donovan, "The Justice of Assignment and Subjective Rights in Grotius," in *Bonds of Imperfection*, ed. Joan Lockwood and Oliver O'Donovan (Grand Rapids: Eerdmans, 2004), 167–201.

37. Ferguson, *Principles*, 185.

38. Ibid., 262.

39. Ibid., 268.

40. Ibid., 457.

41. Ibid., 458.

Nay, but we shall be told, that all men were originally equal. This, in regard to property, can mean only that, when no one had any thing, all men were equally rich: But even this is no more than fancied equality in a single point. In respect to sex and age, strength of body and mind, individuals are destined to inequality from their birth; and, almost in the first steps of society, bear the distinctions which industry and courage give in the different attainments of men, and lead in the sequel to all the varieties of profession and fortune.[42]

Equality, as an ideal, can never be properly deployed or actualized and so therefore should never be made a political aim. Maintaining equality as a political aim would violate the only right every human being *does* hold equally—the right to defend oneself. If the state were to force an ideal of equality it would have to do so at the expense of the only equality society enjoys. Lastly, and perhaps most importantly, liberty cannot consist in the prevalence of democratic power. "The violence of popular assemblies and their tumults need to be restrained, no less than the passions and usurpations of any other power whatever; and there is indeed no species of tyranny under which individuals are less safe than under that of a majority or prevailing faction of a corrupted people."[43] A concert of wills is as susceptible to anarchy and tyranny as a solitary monarch, and thus democracy can neither furnish nor guarantee individual freedom. On the distant view, only attributive justice gives scope to genuine freedom.

In the *Essay*, Ferguson assesses freedom theoretically by comparing ancient (savage) notions with modern. In so doing he names two familiar powers that either restrain or enhance freedom—property and law. Unbridled freedom tends almost universally to corruptions when left to itself. Law mitigates that tendency, however, by instituting the terms of justice. "Where men enjoy peace," he explains, "they owe it either to their mutual regards and affections, or the restraints of law."[44] The greatest threat to civil peace is "desire of lucre," and that prospect requires law to take "a principal reference to property."[45] Paradoxically, the very laws meant to protect against property violations may also instigate further violations, since "many of the establishments which serve to defend the weak from oppression, contribute, by securing the possession of property, to favour its unequal division, and to increase the ascendant of those

---

42. Ibid., 462.
43. Ibid., 464.
44. Ferguson, *Essay*, 150.
45. Ibid.

from whom the abuses of power may be feared."[46] All sorts of provisions have been devised to remedy the problem of unequal property possession but to little avail, revenue caps and abolition of primogeniture being among the more popular policies at the time. Such regulations are scarcely effective. Ferguson understands them to be helpful to commerce initially, but because implemented mainly in countries "whose national object is wealth" the results of policy are inconclusive.[47] Distribution of productive property is crucial, but never decisive.

Insatiable human passions are the real problem. Regulation is "never perfectly attained in any state where the unequal division of property is admitted, and where fortune is allowed to bestow distinction and rank."[48] Regulatory measures are at best coercive. On this point the difference between the ancient and modern on regulating commerce is perhaps most stark. The ancient differs from the modern in that he gives little thought to "possessing" property, because (and Ferguson is behind this commitment wholeheartedly) the ancient "was made to consider himself as the property of his country, not as the owner of a private estate."[49] Genuine patriotism understands fully the permanence of land and concedes to its prevenient authority, submitting humbly in recognition that the land possesses him, not he the land. In political arts every citizen is a part of something larger than himself. But because the modern does not view property possession in the ancient way we should expect blatant economic injustices to persist and for productive property to accumulate in fewer hands. Where the rule of law wavers, freedom is trampled underfoot.

Modern society is manifestly fixated with wealth and with the elevated status attached to it. In modern life everyone is captivated by the promise of commercial gain. The irresistible appeal of commerce, which cajoles society into deep and irrevocable devotion to the ideals of profit and status, leaves its most troubling mark on the institution of labor. In part four of the *Essay*, "Of Consequences that result from the Advancement of Civil and Commercial Arts," Ferguson is at pains to show how commercial progress leads to the separation of professions and to the subsequent "subordination" these divisions establish. "[T]he progress of commerce is but a continued subdivision of the mechanical arts," he tells us; ". . . every species of material is wrought up to the greatest perfection, and every commodity is produced in the greatest abundance."[50] Divisions of labor, in an unsavory irony, bring man and wealth

46. Ibid., 151.
47. Ibid., 152.
48. Ibid.
49. Ibid.

together. But the effect of this division, apart from the plentiful result just described, is that laborers are made "like the parts of an engine, to concur to a purpose without any concert of their own."[51] Ferguson calls this line of work a "mechanical art," since it requires "no capacity" and minimizes personal contribution. In fact, many mechanical arts "require no capacity" and "succeed best under a total suppression of sentiment and reason; and ignorance is the mother of industry as well as of superstition."[52]

With this argument Ferguson levels what is perhaps the first recorded critique of the division of labor. Dividing and redividing the categories of labor refashions the laborer increasingly into a cog; functionally tasked, but devoid of meaning. He points out that manufacturing prospers most "where the mind is least consulted, and where the workshop may, without any great effort of imagination, be considered as an engine, the parts of which are men."[53] The mechanistic reduction of working man to an industrial function might even be described as *inhumane*, treating the worker not as a person but as an instrument of productivity. If this were all Ferguson had to say on the subject our interest would remain piqued, but the division of labor is only the next perplexing phase in the story of commercial advancement.

Division of labor creates the necessary conditions from which the second phase of commercial advancement may proceed: the escalation of subordination. Two types of subordination, or authorial disparities, have already been identified in the *Essay*—natural disparities of talent and unequal divisions of property. Both imply vertical ordering and therefore strain the prospects of true equality. The third type of subordination arises from "the *habits* which are acquired by the practice of different arts."[54] Different occupations make differing contributions to civil society, some more visibly political than others. The work of the judge differs from that of the innkeeper, one irrevocably public and the other mainly private. Each offers a different civic service. Yet what strikes us most about this third subordination is Ferguson's use of the word "habit." Habits acquired from undertaking different occupations lead to still

50. Ibid., 173.

51. Ibid.

52. Ibid., 174.

53. Ibid. Some recent social research has confirmed Ferguson's claim. Researchers at MIT found that (all things being equal), monetary incentives successfully motivate routine mechanical labor, but that when applied to nonmechanical labor requiring any form of rational reflection these same incentives lead actually to *poorer* overall productivity. For a general summary of these case studies on incentivized performance see Daniel H. Pink, *Drive* (New York: Riverhead, 2009).

54. Ferguson, *Essay*, 175.

further subordinations. Each worker's occupation shapes him into something of the occupation's own making. Occupational proficiency thus serves as a lever of stratification. Professions undertaken purely out of intellectual interest and which aim at perfection are considered highest-order occupations, since the worker is not in any sense *bound* to a certain task. In short, an ideal day's work will encourage freedom and creativity, remain non-necessitous by definition, and gravitate ever closer to its ideal. Not everyone is cut out for every variety of work; some prefer the labors of mind while others prefer the labors of hand, but both are needed for the preservation of society.

Equality, the antithesis of subordination, is treated by Ferguson with deep suspicion. The ideal of equality dislodges authority from its traditionally qualitative attribution and levels it categorically. The problem, in other words, is not simply that you and I have equal dignity in the eyes of God but that by nature you and I are equal citizens with equal competencies and contributions. Equality turns the natural verticality of authority horizontal. Excellence, which by definition seeks to surpass the status quo, brings to any political society in search of equality nothing but confusion. If coercion is used to force the ideal, still more political tension is generated, for "[i]f the pretensions to equal justice and freedom should terminate in rendering every class equally servile and mercenary, we make a nation of helots, and have no free citizens."[55] Freedom and equality are *adverse* to one another; the pursuit of freedom transgresses the rules of equality, and the pursuit of equality transgresses the rules of freedom.[56] So, for example, if the state attempts to establish equality as a constitutional principle, then it does so at the expense of certain freedoms. The same goes for freedom—if the state seeks to maximize the freedoms of its citizens it must do so at the expense of citizens' claims to equality.

In their ideal form, freedom and equality are predominantly assessed by their prominence in the commercial sphere. However, it is precisely here, in the commercial sphere, that "the exaltation of the few must depress the many," and freedom descends rapidly into slavery.[57] This occurrence is understood by all to be an injustice without remedy. That "the many" suffer at expense of "the few" has been a long-recognized socio-economic injustice. Some theorists in Ferguson's day seem to have been persuaded that the "meanness" of lower classes arose primarily "from the defect of knowledge and of liberal education."[58]

55. Ibid., 177.

56. For a more contemporary and yet equally compelling treatment of this tension see chapter four of Yves R. Simon's *The Philosophy of Democratic Government* (South Bend, IN: University of Notre Dame Press, 1993).

57. Ferguson, *Essay*, 177.

Late-moderns can therefore take comfort in the knowledge that an argument for educational correction of social deficiencies was a premonition very much alive as early as the mid-eighteenth century! The idea that certain ways of thinking and acting can be educated-out of a general population or that a lack of education is the primary reason for our social woes has been an alluring doctrine for quite some time, it turns out, and in the course of the eighteenth-century debate it was commonly believed that education would elevate the lower class from its distasteful "meanness."

In any event, the main point for our purposes is that the commercial state and the pursuit of equality are antithetical to the liberal state. So antithetical are they, in fact, that the primary objections to democracy itself—the most equalizing political form—are "taken from the inequalities which arise among men in the result of commercial arts."[59] But not for reasons one may assume. For Ferguson, commercial enterprise *disrupts* political representation. "How," he asks, "can he who has confined his views to his own subsistence or preservation be entrusted with the conduct of nations?"[60] Democracy cannot succeed in leveling society because magistrates cannot be trusted to represent their constituents justly. Elected officials being the principal benefactors of nondemocratic commercial arrangements, any hope of sincere parliamentary representation is tenuous at best.

Commercial advancement therefore results in the division of labor and the necessary subordinations resulting from that division. This division and subsequent subordination signals a historical turning point. Latent in the consequences of commercial advancement are the first signs of national decline. But before the reasons for this decline can be articulated he needs first to show how national sentiments are formed and directed. Every nation holds itself in high esteem, and it appears patently evident that "no nation is so unfortunate as to think itself inferior to the rest of mankind: few are even willing to put up with the claim to equality."[61] If one nation sees itself as superior to another it does so according to prejudiced standards. Criteria used to compare qualitative differences between nations must be interrogated, for if the deciding criteria of national greatness are expanded to include achievements harmful to personal or institutional character, then final judgments on the comparative relationship will be fickle at best. "Even where we pretend to found our opinions on reason, and to justify our preference of one nation to another, we frequently bestow our

---

58. Ibid.
59. Ibid., 178.
60. Ibid.
61. Ibid., 194.

esteem on circumstances which do not relate to national character, and which have little tendency to promote the welfare of mankind."[62] Conquest, territory, and wealth are insufficient criteria for determining the character of a nation.

Some theorists will nevertheless contend that wealth and national power are the natural fruits of public virtue, and that loss of these coveted national possessions is a direct result of vice. Prosperity on this view becomes a natural reward for virtue; poverty a natural punishment for vice. For Ferguson, however, it is clear that "the virtues of men have shone most during their *struggles*, not after the attainment of their ends."[63] Virtues display themselves when tried by conflict or resistance, like muscular exercise, and thus disclose the intrinsic quality of an action. The "ends" of wealth and national power are "frequently the causes of corruption and vice," not the prize for virtuous actions.[64] Pushing ever harder for ascendancy among nations—the natural result of what Hume called international "jealousies'"—has brought each to the point of willfully substituting mechanical arts, which increase wealth, for those professions which might benefit the laborer.[65] Identifying national greatness with commercial wealth or prowess betrays the classical—and for that matter *biblical*—view of what it means to be great.

Humility, contentment, and peace are noble qualities that ultimately fail to deliver "commercial advantage" or "national ascendancy." Rich and ascendant societies are "polished," "civilized," and modern; the unpolished are savage and barbarian. Savages and barbarians are peoples who by definition never enjoy the refinements of wealth or national greatness. Nevertheless, both savage and barbarian peoples esteem themselves as great and perhaps even comparably greater than surrounding peoples. Every nation sees itself as great. In asserting a position of prestige, the self-declared "polished" society should be ashamed of its superciliousness. Purportedly "polished" societies would do well to read their history, claims Ferguson, for history shows that "the progress of societies to what we call the heights of national greatness, is not more natural, than their *return* to weakness and obscurity is necessary and unavoidable."[66]

The brutal truth about society is that it is comprised of mere mortals capable of great achievement as well as great failure, and at different times both victim and benefactor of natural circumstance. Greatness is not an artificially contrived or fabricated social status, but a quality only to be *conferred*, never

62. Ibid., 195.
63. Ibid., 196.
64. Ibid.
65. Ibid.
66. Ibid., 198.

demanded. It is perhaps at the exact moment when a society considers itself great that it has actually forsaken the constitutive properties of greatness. This is not to suggest, of course, that one should eliminate all aspirations whatsoever. As we have already seen, the essence of one's life displays itself through exertion. But exertions can also be misdirected or misspent, as is clearly manifest in the pursuit of riches, where "men engage in pursuits with degrees of ardor not proportioned to the importance of their object."[67] The moral question of what end our commercial endeavors pursue is preceded by the question of whether the spirit of progress *itself*, "which for a time continues to carry on the project of civil and commercial arts, find[s] a natural *pause* in the termination of its own pursuits."[68] The word "pause" stands out in that question almost as an absurdity. Pause? Is there ever a chance for progress to pause? Perhaps certain types of progress may allow or even encourage a noticeable pause, but *commercial* progress appears not to be one of these important types. Desire for riches grips the heart and penetrates the soul of every polished nation. The pursuit of wealth is, on Ferguson's account, the beginning of its own unmaking:

> The commercial and lucrative arts may continue to prosper, but they gain an ascendant at the expense of other pursuits. The desire of profit stifles the love of perfection. Interest cools the imagination and hardens the heart; and, recommending employments in proportion as they are lucrative and certain in their gains, it drives ingenuity, and ambition itself to the counter and the workshop. But apart from these considerations, the separation of professions, while it seems to promise improvement of skill, and is actually the cause why the productions of every art become more perfect as commerce advances; yet in its termination and ultimate effects, serves in some measure to *break the bands of society*, to substitute form in place of ingenuity, and to withdraw individuals from the common scene of occupation on which the sentiments of the heart and the mind are most happily employed.[69]

Constant pursuit of interest, refining over and over again the apparatus of production, degrades and devalues the labors of society, breaking it apart

67. Ibid., 202.
68. Ibid., 204 (emphasis mine).
69. Ibid., 206–7.

and forcing it into ever more clandestine occupations. Love of "perfection" and "imagination" are substituted in deference to form and efficiency. This resignation to narrowly defined specializations leads to the common assumption that society is made to consist in parts, "of which none is animated with the spirit of society itself."[70] Such persons as are perilously inattentive to the needs of state, Ferguson follows Pericles in calling "perfectly insignificant."[71] When each is after one's own private interest the broader public interest falls inevitably by the wayside. The state would do well to remain wary of this transition from public to private interest, because it may quickly find its citizens unworthy of the freedoms it protects. It must pay attention, in other words, to the uses being made of freedom. Liberty has its dangers, he reminds us, and people "may be found to grow tired in secret of a free constitution, of which they never cease to boast in their conversation and which they always neglect in their conduct."[72] Public needs are not the concern of Private Man, and this is why "national spirit," that energetic push toward progressive ascendancy among nations, appears frequently transient—the "spirit" of privacy neglects and therefore corrupts the public sphere.[73]

A commercially oriented "national spirit" produces relaxation in, and ignorance of, the shape and necessities of public life. This is for Ferguson the third moment of society's transition toward slavery. "Ordinary establishments," he explains, "terminate in a relaxation of vigor and are ineffectual to the preservation of states; because they lead mankind to rely on their arts, instead of their virtues, and to mistake for an improvement of human nature a mere accession of accommodation or of riches."[74] Packaged covertly into this argument is Ferguson's conviction that every adult male citizen should by law serve in national defense. Pursuing avidly and perhaps unconscionably the social status resulting from wealth leads persons and communities into compromising apathy. "Men frequently, while they study to improve their fortunes, neglect themselves; and while they reason for their country, forget the considerations that most deserve attention." Thus, "a nation consisting of degenerate and cowardly men is weak," asserts Ferguson, and "a nation consisting of a vigorous, public-spirited, and resolute men is strong."[75] This "weak-strong" dichotomy

---

70. Ibid., 207.

71. Ferguson quotes Pericles in part V, section 3 of the *Essay* but does not cite a text.

72. Ferguson, *Essay*, 212.

73. A. O. Hirschman has developed this subtle eighteenth-century tension rather fruitfully, proposing a recurring cycle of public-private attentions. See *Shifting Involvements: Private Interest and Public Action* (Princeton: Princeton University Press, 2002).

74. Ibid.

has origins in antiquity, where the individual who seeks to increase riches and gain greater social prominence is seen as an "effeminate" and corrupted louse, cowardly, unable to possess himself or to wield a weapon. The "strong" citizen who serves the public and humbles himself dutifully on behalf of nation is seen as "heroic," a possessor of "masculine" virtues, a true patriot.

Commercial interest divides the public from private and thus creates conditions for either a weak or strong citizenry. The constant danger is *prioritizing* commercial service to political service. Rigidly dividing professions into narrower fields of precise functionality also deprives citizens of the moral and intellectual resources needed for public service, for "to separate the arts which form the citizen and the statesman, the arts of policy and war, is an attempt to dismember the human character, and to destroy those very arts we mean to improve."[76] This incredible division is interpreted to be a civil "deprivation." Society is thus composed of two distinct classes of citizen: one class has an interest in the preservation of civil establishments but lack the means to defend them, and the other has this power to defend but lacks either the inclination or the interest to do so.[77] Such was the ancient Roman dilemma. It was not until legions became mercenary and fought only for monetary compensation that the proficiency of Roman conquests eroded. This historical insight applies directly to Ferguson's denouncement of standing armies and repeated appeal to establish local militias.

Standing armies of a commercial state are at constant risk of being used as an instrument of commercial *interest*. Just as the mercenaries in Caesar's legions fought for plunder, so too would modern nations fall prey to the lucre of conquest. Warfare couches the moral imperative deceitfully in terms of protecting or promoting interests—lines are constantly blurred, goods distorted, lives lost, and profits made. What was once a service to the public, at least by intention, is given over to each soldier or magistrate's private interest: the publicity of the service masks the true commercial ambitions of the nation. The maintenance of such an army is but an exorbitant "national waste."

The last part of Ferguson's *Essay* brings readers to the argument's final climactic step. National character remains the primary object of his inquiry, only now he shifts his attention to the final corruption incident to the loosening of social bonds and to that corruption's admission of political slavery. Collective focus on the commercial state has settled into the fabric of society like an acid, breaking it apart and dissolving the affections that give it life:

75. Ibid., 213.
76. Ibid., 218.
77. Ibid., 219.

> When mere riches, or court-favour, are supposed to constitute rank; the mind is misled from the consideration of qualities on which it ought to rely. Magnanimity, courage, and the love of mankind, are sacrificed to avarice and vanity, or suppressed under a sense of dependence. The individual considers his community so far only as it can be rendered subservient to his personal advancement or profit: he states himself in competition with his fellow-creatures; and, urged by the passions of emulation, of fear and jealousy, of envy and malice, he follows the maxims of an animal destined to preserve his separate existence, and to indulge his caprice or his appetite, at the expense of his species.[78]

Competition between private interest and public good is therefore the contradictory starting point of the modern commercial state. Citizens tend toward the former, unfortunately, and become either zealous to trespass on others in their rapacious pursuit of profit or willingly relinquish their political privileges for a baser, more servile existence. A nation, as it were, divides naturally into bifurcated roles of either master or slave. The split is "natural" in that it results from a government that views itself principally as a protector and manager of commercial interests. From this management only two parties emerge: "the oppressor who demands, and the oppressed who dare not refuse."[79] The *idea* of Master and Slave does not seem to disturb Ferguson in the slightest; rather, what disturbs him is the prospect of a government blind to obvious injustices:

> Defects of government, and of law, may be in some cases considered as a symptom of innocence and of virtue. But where power is already established, where the strong are unwilling to suffer restraint or the weak unable to find a protection, the defects of law are marks of the most *perfect corruption.* [80]

If the state proves incapable of remedying public injustices, then the moral corruptions of the commercial state have already entrenched themselves in the statutes of law and government, corroding them from within.

78. Ibid., 226.
79. Ibid., 229.
80. Ibid., 230 (emphasis mine).

The source of extravagant corruption and the hidden oracle of national decadence is luxury, which Ferguson defines as "that complicated apparatus which mankind devises for the ease and convenience of life."[81] A luxurious item in one place may not be luxurious in another, and a luxurious advantage in one generation may not be luxurious to the one succeeding it. Conceptions of luxury are in constant flux. Morally disconcerting to Ferguson, however, is the novel *priority* given to luxuries. Whenever a luxurious object "may come to be preferred to friends, to a country, or to mankind," the corruptions of luxury can be seen to have left their mark. And the moral force of luxury "is not to limit men to any particular species of lodging, diet, or clothes; but to prevent their considering these conveniencies as the principal objects of human life."[82] Luxury is by definition a *privileged* possession identified purely by its exclusivity; if a sufficient number possess this "luxurious" object, then it ceases to be luxurious. The luxurious object, to put the matter another way, is one that only *some* people can obtain and when acquired by a sufficient number degrades into an object of mere convenience.

In contemplating this niggling inequality one should bear in mind that the unequal distribution of wealth is a necessary product of any advancing commercial state. A certain level of inequality must be accepted in order to experience any degree of commercial improvement. Luxury is a class concept realized by what the upper class flaunts and lower class envies. Politically this implies that "luxury is . . . *adverse* to the form of democratical government; and in any state of society can be safely admitted in that degree only in which the members of the community are supposed of unequal rank, and constitute public order by means of a regular subordination."[83] Notice the language employed for this distinction—luxury and democracy are not only incompatible with one another but altogether *adverse*. To the extent that democracy implies establishment of equality, or at least the pursuit of equality, luxury will menace the political order with abrupt and irresolvable inequalities. Rulers may recommend one or the other as ends but cannot insist upon both—they are politically incompatible.

Moral corruption is the *prima causa* of institutional corruption. All people are tempted by what they do not presently possess and think unreflectively of felicity consisting in much the way Hobbes describes: "a continual progress of the desire, from one object to another; the attaining of the former, being still

81. Ibid., 231.
82. Ibid., 234.
83. Ibid., 235 (emphasis mine).

but a way to the latter."[84] Regardless of status, whether abiding in cave or palace, everyone longs for sensual gratification in an object not presently possessed. Luxury—that object of near-universal longing—represents a false mirage on the personal and social horizon. When it becomes an object of pursuit, exertive actions have nowhere to go but back upon the actor, amassing upon himself. Ferguson suggests that when left to follow his own private advantages, each will become "effeminate," "mercenary," and "sensual." Yet each will become so not because pleasures and profits have become alluring, "but because he has fewer calls to attend to other objects; and because he has more encouragement to study his personal advantages and pursue his separate interest."[85] Andrew Fletcher, his near predecessor, had also foreseen this danger. Luxury affords some privileged citizens the *choice* of whether to submit to military service or pay the poor to do so for him; "an expensive way of living" that allows the rich to sell the means of freedom and amuse themselves endlessly with private commercial tokens. A luxury of *not* serving martially would seem then to widen the divide between public and private still further.[86]

Self-interested and isolated individuals lose the ability to think and act in service to the public. When this tendency evolves into a widespread national phenomenon, fortune and luxury totalize public attention:

> Nations are most exposed to corruption form this quarter, when the mechanical arts, being greatly advanced, furnish numberless articles to be applied in ornament to the person, in furniture, entertainment, or equipage; when such articles as the rich alone can procure are admired; and when consideration, precedence, and rank are accordingly made to depend on fortune.[87]

The quality of "goodness," the ground of political life, is in turn dissolved into mere appearances—merit and ability become politically superfluous. Within such a society "we rate our fellow-citizens by the *figure* they are able to make," and the highest of our praise is reserved for what seems richest in ostentation. Modern commercial society has thus "transferred the idea of perfection from the character to the equipage; and that excellence itself is, in our esteem, a

---

84. Thomas Hobbes, *Leviathan*, ed. R. Tuck (Cambridge: Cambridge University Press, 1996), 70.

85. Ferguson, *Essay*, 237.

86. See Fletcher's "A Discourse on Government with Relation to Militias" and chapter thirteen of Pocock's *The Machiavellian Moment*, 423–61.

87. Ibid., 238.

mere pageant, adorned at a great expense by the labors of many workmen."[88] And with this observation Ferguson identifies the workings of an informal *bondage*. A rich master uses commoners for commercial and political gain, and the commoners willingly permit their enslavement to "so great" a master. Stocks have hereby snapped shut around the wrists of a nation, although they have not yet been securely locked.

For the corruption of society to achieve completeness, as Fletcher had foreshadowed, commercial society's fascination with luxury must be aided concomitantly by the mass forsaking of public service. The day is coming when otherwise urgent, vital public affairs will be experienced as inconveniences or interruptions to the normal pace of personal enterprise. Under such conditions "the care of mere fortune is supposed to constitute wisdom; retirement from public affairs, and real indifference to mankind, receive the applauses of moderation and virtue."[89] Political life reduces to a series of petty disputes over issues of minor commercial interest. The higher orders of society claim here a particularly cumbersome experience when, in truth:

> They speak of human pursuits, as if the whole difficulty were to find something to do: they fix on some frivolous occupation as if there was nothing that deserved to be done: they consider what tends to the good of their fellow-creatures as a disadvantage to themselves: they fly from every scene, in which any efforts of vigour are required, or in which they might be allured to perform any service to their country.[90]

Who then is truly pitiable? Surely it is not the poor who deserve our pity, insists Ferguson angrily, it is owed more justly to the rich! In their lavish inactivity they waste away on novel indulgences and fresh sensualities all while disaffected by concerns of others. Political society's situation is therefore dismal.

Portrayed thusly the modern commercial state can only terminate in political slavery. This slavery is two-tiered: slavery within the society itself, where the upper class rules the lower by virtue of fortune and status, and slavery between nations. The latter form is foreshadowed randomly throughout earlier parts of the *Essay* and is only made explicit at the argument's climax. National

88. Ibid., 239.
89. Ibid., 243.
90. Ibid., 246.

slavery occurs when fortune ceases to be used as an instrument for good and becomes instead the *idol* of a slackened and sickened public conscience. Fortune, "the foundation on which freedom was built, may serve to support a *tyranny*; and what, in one age, raised the pretensions, and fostered the confidence of the subject, may, in another, incline him to servility, and furnish the price to be paid for his prostitutions."[91] Wealth enhances freedom preliminarily, but when popularly admired "leads to *despotical government.*"[92] Riches become so singularly exalted in public life that the rule of law itself is bent by the anarchic forces of interest to conceal rather than restrain the "iniquities of power." Law is the soil that gives life to genuine liberty, but if the soil is disparaged and the roots of freedom maimed, then each citizen must be willing to vindicate his own freedom for himself. Under a private commercial state, therefore, "even political establishments . . . cannot be relied on for the preservation of freedom."[93]

Ferguson understands that in the long run, higher orders of society will begin to revere one another in much the same way the lower order of society reveres the higher. Each will be prepared to do whatever it takes to ascend the social ladder, especially if all it requires is feigned (or real) admiration of those who stand in position to benefit. So long as one's money-making capacities remain unimpeded it does not matter whether wealth becomes increasingly isolated in fewer hands or whether a solitary individual controls the political sword.

Here we see the undercurrent of Ferguson's argument come full circle—he is mindful of militias and the establishment of a standing army at royal disposal. When the division between public and private is formally established, separating civilian and public professions, the way is prepared for a "dangerous alliance of faction with military power."[94] Soon *conquest* becomes a political end in itself, and as was the case for ancient Rome, so it will be in modern Britain:

> In proportion as territory is extended, its parts lose their relative importance to the whole. Its inhabitants cease to perceive their connection with the state, and are seldom united in the execution of any national, or even factious, designs. Distance from the seats of administration, and indifference to the persons who contend for

91. Ibid., 248 (emphasis mine).
92. Ibid.
93. Ibid., 251.
94. Ibid., 256.

preferment, teach the majority to consider themselves as the subjects of a sovereignty, not as the members of a political body.[95]

Conquest reinforces the perception of dissociation. Of all the consequences tendered by the modern commercial state, it is "perpetual enlargement of territory" that leads most naturally to despotism. Even the government in a political situation of complete commercialization and national servitude takes a view to its own fiscal interests, where it becomes (like its subjects) devoted to the protection and promotion of its *own* commercial interests. The irony, illustrated vividly by the history of civil society itself, is that to conquer and to be conquered often appears the same, sharing in the same ultimate conclusion. *Slavery* is the political, social, and personal outcome of the commercial state. Each citizen is either enslaved to his own desires, to the empowered elites of his community, or to the despotic ruler of state: "Obedience is the only duty that remains, and this is exacted by force."[96] Enslavement concludes the tragic narrative of commercial society paradoxically by reaching its historical climax with a conquest that is always also its anticlimax. For although conquest might appear the apex of political power it is in fact the genesis of impotence and enslavement; speaking not of power, but of uncertainty; expressing nothing of contentment or peace, but of ambition, greed, and capriciousness.

The observation that interior slavery carries political consequences is by no means original. This powerful biblical concept serves as a central theme in the Old Testament narrative of ancient Israel, which the apostle Paul identifies and exploits rather ably in his epistles, and then is expounded upon insightfully by Augustine and amenable commentators standing downstream from him. Ferguson's originality consists in having recognized the unique role played by the liberal economy in facilitating slavery. The economy plays a functional role in establishing political slavery. Just how clairvoyant his claims are will be the subject of our next chapter.

95. Ibid.
96. Ibid., 259.

5

Trappings of Liberal Democratic Capitalism

Today's economic situation is an embarrassment in both the contemporary and historical senses of the term. We hold our collective blush at each new revelation of foreclosures, corporate layoffs, debt spikes, insider trading, and corporate scandal. Embarrassment in the *historic* sense, moreover, with its medieval allusion to "entanglement" or "obstruction," signals for us a deeper, less sentimental impediment. Transgressions in modern commerce having been publicly exposed, we recognize, for all our cherished freedom, that much of economic life has become entangling and obstructive. Contemporary societies are not entirely unlike quicksand victims flailing in panic; regretful of having wandered mindlessly into the pit, we thrash about only to achieve deeper and more troubling distresses. *Man does not know his time*, reminds the writer of Ecclesiastes, *like fish caught in a treacherous net and birds caught in a snare, so the sons of men are ensnared at an evil time when it suddenly falls on them* (Eccles. 9:12).

The success of traps depends, of course, on their being unforeseen. If modern economic pursuits have led us into embarrassing snares, this experience raises the natural question of what kinds of moral and political contradiction the emancipatory efforts of modern commerce introduce to societies. And likewise, to carry our metaphor but one step further, invites us to consider *how* the ensnarement so described is to be reconciled with the overarching secular demand for modern capital-economies to remain characteristically emancipatory.

Ferguson's history of civil society displays clear understanding of the moral and political compromises inherent to commercial enterprise. Posing ancient Greek and Roman societies as examples, he demonstrates how a distinctly modern understanding of commercial interest creates both moral and political contradictions. Societies overly occupied with the pursuit of wealth become submissive to the point of defenseless, and when unable or unwilling to preserve domestic order are easily dominated by a foreign power. A commercial society is effectively incapacitated. This is what he means when he says that fortune may come to support a tyrant—the very object of pursuit becomes the catalyst for political domination.

He does not appear to have noticed it himself, but inherent to the logic of Ferguson's argument is the crucial premise that *the liberal pursuit of wealth in commercial enterprise undermines political institutions*. He has in mind an assertive military despot who marches without resistance into a territory and seizes all political control. Having expended all its energies in the pursuit of commercial gain, the rich nation forfeits its ability to make war and thus succumbs to the power of a nation that can. As late-moderns standing centuries removed, we must resist the urge to discount Ferguson's argument as primitive or naïve. Surmising impulsively that his situation was so very different from our own or that questions faced in eighteenth-century Britain could not possibly correspond to political questions of the early twenty-first century are equally naïve. *Are* they so different? Do we not detect something poignant and applicable in Ferguson's historical assessment of commercial society? What Ferguson could *not* have seen when modern capitalism was but a sapling in the great forest of political history was how and to what degree that sapling would mature and eventually seed itself across the globe. He *could* see that the progress of democratic capitalism gradually undermines political institutions, as was already patently evident in the dispassionate view of military service among social elites, but we have in our time seen his claim come true in an altogether different way.

In our age we have watched the *market itself* become the tyrant. If one permits this personification—and there is little reason for disallowing it, seeing as the commonest references to "the market" are in regard to its "habits," "moods," and "reactions"—then it is relatively clear that the Market can, in fact, *tyrannize*. Market tyranny asserts itself temperamentally and often without political or legal repercussion. On a political level the marketplace appears at times both constructive and destructive; it replenishes tax revenues for the building of infrastructure, for instance, while at the same time bringing productive property into the hands of a shrinking number of benefactors. Moral and political inconsistencies associated with health care, or campaign finance, or real estate, or investment banking, for example, emerge as each distinct market tends to moral or political extremes when configured by capitalist logic: the commodification of health, buying of votes, opposition to reform, and reimbursement of stock gamblers. Political institutions are therefore either intrinsically broken or simply prone to commercial domination. Ferguson, for his part, had already detected this impulse latent in the history of society—political society accommodates the market's will naturally, although the market's demand for political attention is not itself a brand of tyranny. The market becomes genuinely tyrannical only when it destroys or forsakes the very political institutions meant to govern it, stampeding them underfoot as a violent herd shatters its picket corral.

To late eighteenth-century and early nineteenth-century theorists who would view the dawning of liberal capitalism as the initial victory of democracy over monarchy as a political form, Ferguson has already rejoined with at least two reasons why this usurpation would not be successful. First, when wealth is made the principal object of commercial pursuit, a dual slavery is formalized—between possessors and dispossessed, and also between nations. Slavery is total. If one were not at all enslaved to riches, then one would be enslaved to another who is; if one society were to become intoxicated by the pleasures of riches, then it would be quickly enslaved by another society virtuous enough to resist the same temptation.

Slavery is total because greed appears unavoidably pervasive, made possible by way of a simple idea that has gradually bewitched the modern world: *Luxury*. Luxury, as we have seen, relies for its existence on class divisions because it is defined by enjoyments premised on exclusivity. When a luxury becomes the possession of enough non-elites the object or service no longer remains a luxury but instead degrades into a mere convenience. Luxury therefore abolishes any prospect of equality. Equality is impossible in free market societies animated by the multiplication of wealth, because wealth by its very existence drives a wedge between those who possess the means of productive property and those who do not.[1] How then, Ferguson asks, can a legitimate democratic government be established upon such conditions? When the object of commercial exchange leads to deeper inequalities why should anyone expect democratic processes to endure?

In supposed representative democracies of the early twenty-first century, political power is not—contrary to popular opinion—held by that collection of individuals comprising the majority, but by those who possess the greatest monetary resources, who, in order to command political control must *first* be market beneficiaries *prior* to becoming political magistrates. This problem offers two revelations. The first is the patently obvious reality of civic representatives

---

1. For a useful historical overview of luxury as a concept, see Christopher J. Berry, *The Idea of Luxury* (Cambridge: Cambridge University Press, 1994).

being faced with a conflict-of-interest between economic gains and political service. Who are representatives to support, for example, when a piece of legislation creates tension between the interests of a party-supporting multinational corporation and those of the wider electorate? Whose needs are being represented? This phenomenon poses a perennial dilemma. Constituents cannot control whom or to what their magistrates will lend support. Second, and perhaps the more important revelation, is a profound blindness to forces giving rise to political power as such. Elections are won these days by the savvy and solvent, for it is apparent that candidates must first hold exceptional wealth in order to hold political appointment. It turns out political authority of the democratic variety comes with a price. Nevertheless, when it is finally recognized that possession of wealth has become a necessary condition to the acquisition of political power, the undermining of political institutions by the Market has become complete, for when wealth becomes the primary means to political power the object of societal corruption has itself become *institutionalized*.

If slavery is an institution—not "slavery" in the modern sense of physical and psychological cruelty, but in the ancient sense of *servus*, or service—and commercial order is defined largely by the relationships humans share with one another in the exchange of wares, then it means a great deal that Ferguson joins a host of early-modern theorists in referring to market exchanges as "commerce," drawing as it does from the Latin tradition of "coming together" to swap merchandise. The marketplace was not yet an abstraction, but instead a collection of real people coming together to trade tangible objects. On these terms Locke was correct in suggesting a permanent link between the vitality of commerce and the labors that go into it; labor and land are indeed partners in the genesis of commerce. But if labor is always a necessary pillar of commerce this means everyone must render service to someone: masters serve slaves, as it were, and slaves serve their masters. "Everyone is a slave to someone" would seem to be an essential human aphorism that on the commercial level smacks of universal truth.[2] Society's fundamental composition is premised on the tacit offering and acceptance of service. Yet, at the same time, we realize that despite a master's service to slave, there is a distinguishable "slave class" in society, a larger proportion of slaves who labor on behalf of a smaller proportion of masters. Marx, of course, found this to be the Injustice of all injustices. But what

---

2. For all its historical fascination, on this point Hilaire Belloc came up short. The capitalist and the collectivist were moral menaces to modern society, to be sure, but their theoretical tendency to a "servile state" misjudges the historical fact that slavery is a permanent human fixture, not simply a recurring adjustment. See *The Servile State* (London: Constable & Co., 1948).

we have seen in the latter twentieth and early twenty-first centuries is a further impoverishment of this relationship. If it is true that slavery is an institution, as has been suggested, what distinguishes the late-modern slave is her noticeable deprivation of *service*, since it seems there is no denying that the late-modern slave now has little knowledge of *who*, exactly, her master is, and if that were not enough, the work assigned to her is even *less* meaningful.[3] Modern slave-labor is very typically dedicated to corporate multinationals owned by masters without faces or names; it is from the slave's perspective service only to an idea or possibility. The labors undertaken, moreover, are often fragmented the moment they are completed, circulated numerically to different departments and then tallied as a percentage in stock value. On rare occasion these same slaves are offered stock options affording them limited "ownership" in the business their efforts serve, collectable by installments upon retirement. Still, the fact remains that the slave is required daily to continue button-clicking and data-plugging without the slightest prospect of imagination, service, or sense of purpose. Deprived of soul, slavery defined effectively by service is emptied of content, unmaking itself as the *object* or purpose of service becomes increasingly obscured.

Ferguson's theoretical conclusion, at any rate, is that the society pursuant of commercial gain as its principal object will become weak and susceptible to domination and enslavement. He is concerned, in other words, with what riches *do* to people and the political ramifications incurred. Commerce aimed at multiplying wealth undermines political institutions—that is the crux of Ferguson's argument. It was this political principle, aided by the fortunate position of being over two centuries removed, that allowed us to make a contemporary application: the liberalized market bent on the pursuit of wealth undermines political institutions to such an extent that it seems now in its highly abstract and personified form to have *itself* become the tyrant Ferguson anticipated. By extension, the modern market economy is also adverse to democratic government. This adversity endures because of luxury, which drives a wedge into society by fostering tensions and conflicts that disintegrate prospects of equity within the political order. Luxury is premised on inequality, and so long as luxury remains part of capitalism's project the level of social equality required for genuine democratic order will never be reached. And this is precisely why, despite the murderous efforts of revolutionaries, history

---

3. As alluded to in chapter 3, members of the "creative class" are here exempt from this loose categorization, since, depending on the nature of their labor, their production is routinely tangible and their service to the common good more readily apparent.

has never seen a pure democratic government. Freedom and equality prove themselves an incompatible couple.

In a world comprised of errant human beings even the mightiest establishments are susceptible to crimes of ruin. Civil authorities appointed to protect us from ourselves cannot forever withstand the belligerent corruptions repeatedly foisted upon them. Ferguson was correct in seeing slavery at the heart of commercial and political life. In each sphere we find items to bind and possess, like people or land, just as we also find items that bind us, like law and families. Absolute freedom is eternally relegated to the realm of ideas, never to be actualized—until the coming of the Kingdom, that is, when final Judgment releases freedom from the dark bondage constraining its glory. Until that Judgment, humanity must live with the institutions it has been given *and be subject to the governing authorities* (Rom. 13:1). Those authorities are appointed by God as ministers to the people, of course, and Paul goes on to remind the Romans that they need only fear a magistrate if they do wrong, *for he beareth not the sword in vain* (13:4). The coercive power of political authority is necessary for the correction of evil, of righting wrongs, and yet the clause "*he beareth not the sword in vain*" seems to imply a mild disbelief in the coercive prowess of rulers. If confidence in the talent of authorities to restrain evil wanes it must be temporary, thinks Paul, since the sword *cannot* be wielded in vain. But what are we then to do with the *perception* of political impotence? When society is visited by egregious wrongdoing and the authorities fail to rectify it, why is one unjustified in believing their rulers *vain*?

Ferguson's historically oriented political theory seems to assume that a fully commercial state succumbs to vanity in both senses of the word—in its arrogance and in its impotence. To ensure the breadth and acceleration of domestic prosperity, governing authorities are incentivized to protect interests abroad and to rely in turn upon widespread and often elaborate military campaigns. Domestic economy animates foreign policy. So, far from eliminating international armed conflict as Hume so confidently hoped, prolonged fixation with wealth acquisition upsets foreign relations. War might even be waged for purely economic reasons. When economic growth at home overwhelms foreign policy or indeed justifies otherwise warrantless aggression, that nation has exhibited one vain tendency: to view other nations as essentially serviceable to commercial interests, even to the point of compromising on principle.

The mate to this exterior form of vanity is the ulterior form of national impotence. By characterizing the commercial state as especially vulnerable to moral corruption, Ferguson establishes himself among the earliest historians to chronicle the origins of modern decadence. The economically obsessed society is vain in this second sense because it has forfeited the capacity to serve public ends or to rally martially in its defense should the need arise. Domestic impotence is therefore the thesis to which foreign arrogance is the antithesis: the dialectic is mutually informing and supportive yet destined to self-destruct. Domestic luxury prompts foreign aggression and foreign aggression prompts further domestic luxury, a vicious cycle that must inevitably collapses upon itself. Vanity in both its expressions epitomizes the modern commercial state.

In all these respects contemporary configurations of the market economy are an overt embarrassment. The current functions of the Market ensnare us by undermining the institutions meant to secure our path. Ferguson's depiction of commercial society's succumbing to political slavery hints therefore at the following idea: the emancipating efforts of modern economy make it the principal *vehicle of secularization*. Undermining the institutions meant to order it, liberal democratic capitalism carries forward the projects of secularization with bewildering efficiency and deception, the necessary components for any decent trap. The argument here is decidedly biblical in character, for it assumes the truth of Paul's instruction to Timothy in chapter six verse ten of 1 Timothy: *But those who desire to be rich fall into temptation, into a snare, into many senseless and hurtful desires that plunge men into ruin and destruction. For the love of money is the root of all evil; it is through this craving that some have wandered away from the faith, and pierced their hearts with many pangs.*

Index